BERLITZ®

STOCKHOLM

 By the staff of Berlitz Guides

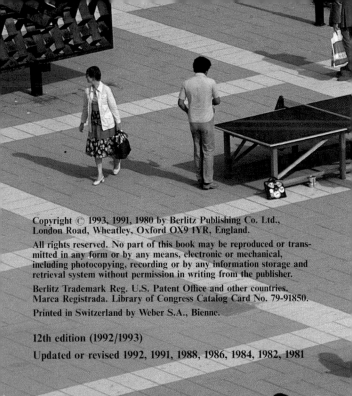

12th edition (1992/1993)

Updated or revised 1992, 1991, 1988, 1986, 1984, 1982, 1981

How to use our guide

- All the practical information, hints and tips that you will need before and during the trip start on page 103.

- For general background, see the sections The City and Its People, p. 6, and A Brief History, p. 15.

- All the sights to see are listed between pages 28 and 63, with suggestions on excursions from Stockholm from page 63 to 79. Our own choice of sights most highly recommended is pinpointed by the Berlitz traveller symbol.

- Entertainment, nightlife and other leisure activities are described between pages 79 and 92, while information on restaurants and cuisine is to be found on pages 94 to 102.

- Finally, there is an index at the back of the book, pp. 126–128.

Found an error or an omission in this Berlitz Guide? Or a change or new feature we should know about? Our editor would be happy to hear from you, and a postcard would do. Be sure to include your name and address, since in appreciation for a useful suggestion, we'd like to send you a free travel guide. Write to: Berlitz Publishing Company Ltd., London Road, Wheatley, Oxford OX9 1YR, England.

Although we make every effort to ensure the accuracy of all the information in this book, changes occur incessantly. We cannot therefore take responsibility for facts, prices, addresses and circumstances in general that are constantly subject to alteration.

Text: Edward Maze
Photography: Jean-Claude Vieillefond
Layout: Aude Aquoise
For their help in the preparation of this book, we wish to thank the Swedish Tourist Board, particularly Thérèse Andersson, Karl Wellner, and Christina Guggenberger of the Stockholm Information Service. We're also grateful to the Scandinavian Airlines System and John H. Herbert for their assistance. Additional photos: pp. 6–7, PRISMA/Kündig; pp. 84 and 89, Swedish Tourist Board; p. 91, PRISMA/Brännhage.
Cartography: (Falk) Falk-Verlag, Hamburg

Contents

Maps

The City and Its People

An ambitious building programme has literally changed the face of Stockholm. In the centre of this 700-year-old city, classic towers and turrets have given way to new buildings with roofs as flat as pancakes. Offices have replaced apartments, forcing many former residents out to the mushrooming suburbs. Of Greater Stockholm's 1.4 million population, fewer than 700,000 live in the city proper.

Stockholm's contemporary configuration is epitomized by Sergels Torg, named after the 18th-century Swedish sculptor Johan Tobias Sergel. But the artist, who had a studio in this district, would scarcely recognize the place. The focal point of the new Stockholm, Sergels Torg now sports a multi-million dollar shopping mall. It has also become the city's main protest centre, where speakers rage against the tyranny of foreign dictators, cry out in favour of gay rights and women's lib, demand more day-care centres for tots and so on in an often carnival-like atmosphere.

To begin with, Stockholm is widely acknowledged as one of the world's most beautiful

cities. Dramatically situated at a point where the cobalt blue of Lake Mälaren meets and clashes with the darker hue of the Baltic Sea, the city has been splendidly endowed by nature. It sprawls gracefully over 14 islands connected by no fewer than 40 bridges. Swedish novelist Selma Lagerlöf described Stockholm, most aptly, as "the city that floats on water."

To complete the picture, one should mention the green

parks and flower-filled squares, church steeples silhouetted against a mauve midsummer sky, narrow lanes and wide quayside boulevards for strollers, billowing sailboats and motorboats dotting the channels and the archipelago, which starts at the city's doorstep.

Stockholm had to wait almost 400 years before becoming Sweden's capital in 1634. Growth was painfully slow until the middle of the 19th century. Today the city is not only

Futuristic dome in southern area of Stockholm, the Globe Arena, is gigantic stadium and concert hall.

the seat of the national parliament and of the royal palace, but also the country's financial and business centre. And though there's plenty of elbow room in Sweden, the fourth largest country in Europe, more than one-sixth of the population crowds into the Stockholm area.

7

Young street musicians add a colourful note to many parts of the city.

The different islands and districts that make up Stockholm are often so unlike one another that they create the illusion of a series of miniature and only distantly related cities. Each has its own distinct charm and mood.

Take Gamla Stan, the Old Town, for instance. In this island of antiquity in the heart of **8** the city, Stockholm first saw the light of day around 1252. Walking along its cobbled alleys and twisting lanes, flanked by perfectly preserved 15th- and 16th-century houses, some with copper roofs, takes you back to medieval times.

By way of contrast, Norrmalm, the northern sector of town, represents the world of the late 20th century—the glass skyscrapers, shopping malls,

underpasses, overpasses and traffic circles of the city centre. Adjoining Norrmalm is Östermalm, a fashionable neighbourhood of stately apartment buildings where many foreign embassies are located.

Kungsholmen, the island just west of the city centre, plays host to the municipal administration. The area is graced by the strikingly handsome Stadshuset (City Hall), rising on the shore of Lake Mälaren.

For yet another facet of

Sweden: Facts and Figures

Geography. Area 173,732 square miles, slightly larger than California, somewhat smaller than Spain. Situated on the Scandinavian peninsula in northern Europe, Sweden borders on Norway and Finland. There are mountains to the north, flat or rolling terrain in the central and southern areas. Half the country is forested. Bay and headlands indent the rocky coastline, and many islands lie offshore.

Population: 8.5 million. Over 80 per cent of the people live in cities (1,400,000 in the capital of Stockholm). Aside from the Swedish majority, three per cent are Finnish and the remainder European immigrants and Lapps (Sami).

Government. Constitutional monarchy headed by King Carl XVI Gustaf (head of state) and a prime minister (head of government). Legislation rests with the unicameral *Riksdag* of 349 members elected for three-year terms.

Economy. Major industries include steel, machinery, instruments, autos, shipbuilding, paper. Wood pulp and paper products account for a quarter of all exports.

Language. Swedish.

Religion. Lutheran (95%).

Stockholm have a look at Söder, the huge, hilly southern island overlooking the rest of the city. Its lofty location and many artist studios give Söder a kind of Montmartre atmosphere. You'll also find charming clusters of old wooden cottages in rural-like settings.

Stockholm spends a great deal of money to beautify the city and maintain its extensive recreational areas. One million flowers are planted every year in the municipal parks, which feature 9,000 park benches, 150 bird-feeding stations, 150 playgrounds for children and 30 open-air stages, where ballet, drama, band concerts and folk dances are presented free of charge during the summer months. And more than 500 sculptures, bought by the city, adorn parks and squares all over town.

Cultural life in Stockholm thrives as never before, in particular the performing arts, which receive large national

Harmonious houses perch like building blocks on the cliffs of Söder, Stockholm's huge southern island. The view's also good from on high.

and municipal subsidies. Public money supports the 200-year-old Royal Opera, one of the best in the world, the excellent Royal Dramatic Theatre and many more. And the city boasts over 50 museums.

Stockholm can also lay claim to having the world's longest art gallery: the city underground transport system, which extends over almost 100 kilometres. The walls and ceilings of many of its stations are decorated with paintings, stone and inlaid glass mosaics, sculpture and other art forms. It's worth a ride on the underground, even if you don't have any special place to go.

11

At one time nightlife was pratically non-existent in Stockholm, but along with the new architecture came a virtual explosion of nightclubs, pubs and discotheques. The city now swings after dark. Eating habits have also changed, with foreign cuisine—Chinese, French, Italian and others—replacing traditional Swedish food in many restaurants. This culinary switch is due, in part, to the big influx of foreign workers but also to the fact that Swedes, who enjoy a minimum five-week, fully paid vacation, are travelling abroad in increasing numbers and acquiring new tastes in food.

A glance at shop windows, or at the people on the street, confirms that this is a very affluent city. Stockholmers live well and dress well—with the exception of teenagers, who have their own views on what "good dressing" is. In the stores you'll find the best of Sweden's famous design products, including superb crystal from the glassworks district of Småland in the south-eastern part of the country.

What about the Swedes themselves? One could generalize by saying they are a very pragmatic, orderly and perhaps overly reserved people with a strong sense of social consciousness. They have put many innovative, humane laws on the books that have become models for the world. If the Swedes appear to be very materialistic, they also remain close to nature. The average Swedish home may be over-equipped with kitchen gadgets, but comes summer and the family retreats to its modest *stuga*, or cottage, in a rustic woodland setting for a taste of the simple life. And from July to September, armies of berry pickers and mushroom hunters invade the forests.

As a summer city, Stockholm—and especially its lovely environs—is hard to beat. Tourist sightseeing boats glide under the city's bridges, white steamers sweep through the wonderful island labyrinth of the Baltic archipelago or head for Drottningholm and Gripsholm, two marvellous palaces on the outer shores of Lake Mälaren. There is music and dancing in the parks, concerts at the Royal Palace, recitals in many of the museums and churches. And everything—water, bridges, squares, steeples—is bathed in the eerily beautiful midsummer light.

You shouldn't get the idea, however, that Stockholm is worth visiting only in the summer. There are some people who admire the city most when newly fallen leaves turn Strandvägen into an avenue of autumn colours, or when the buds burst violently in Haga and other parks in the spring. The city can be enchanting in the dead of winter, too, when the snow makes picture post-cards out of narrow lanes and tiny squares, and bays, channels and canals freeze over solidly, allowing Stockholmers to walk and ski over roads and white fields that were summer waterways and inlets of the sea.

Stockholm has something to offer the visitor in every season.

On Midsummer, Swedish girls wear garlands of flowers in their hair.

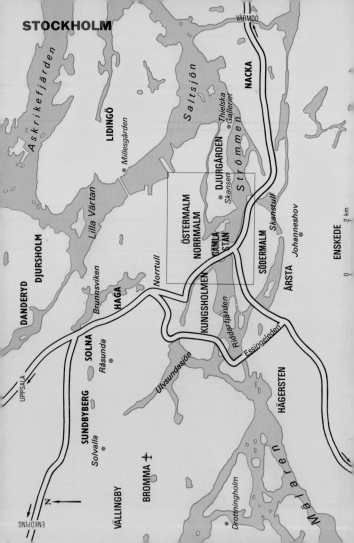

A Brief History

Swedish history begins somewhere around 12,000 B.C.—at any rate, this is what archaeologists have established as the time when the miles-thick blanket of ice covering the whole country started to melt. In the subsequent millennia, nomadic tribes of hunters and fishermen followed the receding ice cap northwards to Sweden. About 3000 B.C., it seems, the inhabitants were cultivating the land, raising livestock and living together in communities.

Magnificent Bronze Age relics, including weapons and ornaments, indicate an early period of prosperity. Mysterious rock carvings of animals and people also remain from that period. But by the time Swedes, as such, are mentioned for the first time in recorded history, conditions had changed quite a bit. This was in A.D. 98, in *Germania*, where Roman historian Tacitus described these ancestors of the Vikings as fierce warriors with mighty fleets.

The Vikings

Sweden remained relatively isolated for a long period. But, in due course, the civilized countries to the south became painfully aware of the Nordic barbarians. The Viking Age, which lasted from about A.D. 800 to 1050, was wild and bloody. Some of the battles and exploits of this time are recorded on the thousands of rune stones to be found in Sweden.

History remembers the Vikings best for their ferocious raids on countries that were better off. They simply helped themselves to what they wanted rather than attempting to eke out an existence in their harsh homeland.

However, the popular image of the Vikings as the villains in history—as bloodthirsty warriors who found pleasure in looting, rape and murder—has been undergoing revision. Modern scholarship has revealed that the Vikings were also remarkable poets and artists, explorers and settlers who made many positive contributions to the territories they occupied. In their famous long ships, manned by as many as 50 oarsmen, these extraordinary seamen pushed west to England, Ireland and Scotland, overran large areas of France, established new colonies in the Faroes, Iceland and Greenland, and finally reached the shores of North America. The Swedish Vikings, who turned towards the east, travelled along the rivers of Russia, es- **15** tablishing control over Novgorod and Kiev, and went on as far as Constantinople.

The navigational skills of the Vikings, moreover, equipped them admirably for far-flung trading expeditions, and they became merchants as well as marauders. Commercial considerations eventually induced these heathens to turn to religion so as to be on a more equal footing with the Christian countries.

Early Christianity

Throughout the Viking period, Christian missionaries, mostly English and German monks, were active in Sweden. The first Christian church was founded about 830 in Birka (on an island in Lake Mälaren) by Ansgar, a monk from Picardie.

Christianizing Sweden was an uphill battle, to say the least, and there were sporadic lapses into paganism as late as

History in the Field

Sweden's elongated landscape—stretching about a thousand miles from north to south—can be compared to a vast open-air museum amply furnished with fascinating artefacts from the dim past.

First and foremost are the Viking rune stones, several thousand of them scattered throughout the country in fields, wooded areas, along roads and highways. These strange memorials record history and perpetuate myths. Their hieroglyphics and picture-writing recount the ancestry, the everyday and heroic moments of the Viking warriors for whom the rune stones were raised. Roughly half of them are located in the province of Uppland, just north of the Swedish capital, and a fine selection are on display in the National Historical Museum in Stockholm (see p. 59).

Other prominent features of the landscape dating from far-off times include cromlechs (stone burial enclosures), fabulous rock carvings of boats, animals and people and Viking burial mounds.

Best of all, perhaps, are the medieval country churches found all over Sweden. The Baltic island of Gotland alone has over 90 of them. Filled with remarkably well-preserved naïve wood sculptures, stained glass windows, altar paintings and murals by local craftsmen, these lovely churches reflect provincial attitudes toward religion and life. They are as fascinating as they are numerous and form an integral part of the Swedish countryside.

the 12th century. In Uppsala, for instance, yearly sacrificial feasts were held in honour of the Norse gods. By the 13th century, however, the church had become a dominant force in the country. The first archbishop, with a diocese in Uppsala, was appointed in 1164, and many churches were built during this period.

In the 13th century, a time of strife and contending factions, the dominant figure to emerge was Birger Jarl. Brother-in-law of the king, he promoted a strong central government and encouraged trade with other nations. When the king died, Birger Jarl had his own son elected heir to the throne. He is also credited with

Rune stones bearing messages from Viking times dot the countryside.

the founding of Stockholm in 1250 or thereabouts as a fort to protect against pirate raids.

The outstanding personality of the following century was St. Birgitta, a religious mystic who gained international fame. Born in 1303, this remarkable woman was a prominent court figure, wife of a nobleman and mother of eight children. She founded a monastic order and church in the town of Vadstena in central Sweden, and her book *Revelations,* translated into Latin and widely read throughout the Christian world, is considered a masterpiece of medieval literature. St. Birgitta died in Rome, but her remains were brought back to Vadstena and buried in the church there.

The Kalmar Union

To counteract the growing power of the German Hanseatic League, the so-called Kalmar Union (named after the Swedish city where the document was signed) was formed in 1397. It united Sweden, Denmark and Norway under a single ruler, the very able Queen Margareta of Denmark, making it Europe's largest kingdom.

The Swedes came in time to resent the dominance of the

GVSTAF VASA.   OSCAR II.

ARX GRIPSHOLM

1537   1892

Singularly shaped medieval bell-tower of Gamla Uppsala church; a stained-glass window in Gripsholm honours two of Sweden's kings.

Danes and many were opposed to the union. In the 1430s they were led in a popular rebellion by the great Swedish hero Engelbrekt, who also assembled the first Swedish parliament in 1435. This Riksdag, which included representatives of the four estates—nobles, clergy, burghers and peasants—elected Engelbrekt regent of Sweden. But soon afterwards he was murdered and the unpopular union limped along until 1520.

That was the year the Scandinavian monarch, Christian II of Denmark, ruthlessly executed scores of Swedish noblemen. These opponents of **19** his rule had been accused of heresy. But instead of eliminating the undercurrent of revolt, the "Stockholm Blood Bath" set off a popular reaction that ended in the disintegration of the despised Union of Kalmar.

One of the noblemen who escaped death, Gustav Vasa, called on the peasants of the province of Dalarna to rebel against the Danish tyrant. With a ragtag army supported by foreign mercenaries, he succeeded in routing the Danes. He was crowned king in 1523 at the age of 27, and his dynamic reign dominated the 16th century.

Gustav Vasa was a strong-willed leader who reshaped the nation, earning him the sobriquet "Father of His Country". He reorganized the state administration and stabilized its finances by, among other things, confiscating all of the church's very considerable property holdings. He also backed the Reformation forces in Sweden as a means of curbing ecclesiastical power. The Swedish church broke with Rome and the Lutheran religion was officially adopted. Three of his sons ruled Sweden after Gustav Vasa died in 1560, and the Vasa dynasty continued for almost 150 years.

Sweden as a World Power

Foremost of the Vasa kings was Gustavus Adolphus, crowned in 1611 at the age of 17. He promoted trade and industry, strengthened the hand of parliament and extended the borders of Sweden by conquests in Russia and Poland. Under his forceful leadership

Sweden became, for a time, the greatest power in 17th-century Europe.

But perhaps it could be considered a portent of things to come that in 1628 the imposing warship Wasa (see p. 46), a fitting symbol of a mighty nation, sank in the Stockholm harbour on her maiden voyage. And then, a few years after this calamity, Gustavus Adolphus

(see p. 46)

With its formal gardens, sweeping lawns, many statues and fountains, 17th-century Drottningholm is often called the Versailles of Sweden.

was killed in battle in Germany, defending the Protestant cause in the Thirty Years' War.

As his daughter Kristina was only six when Gustavus Adolphus died, the extremely capable Count Axel Oxenstierna served as regent. Kristina was crowned in 1644. A very gifted but eccentric woman, she made her court a brilliant salon, inviting to Sweden many famous intellectuals, such as the French philosopher Descartes. Stockholm began to evolve from a rustic village into an elegant city. Ten years later the queen startled the nation by abdicating. She converted to Catholicism and eventually settled in Rome.

During the 17th century Sweden (which had previously annexed Estonia) gained additional ground in the Baltic and along the German coasts. It also extended its borders into parts of Denmark and Norway. Overseas, Sweden established its first colony in the United States in what is now Delaware.

Sweden's last period as a great power occurred under Charles XII, who became monarch of the realm in 1697 at the age of 15. He is one of the most celebrated and controversial figures in the history of Sweden. Encouraged by a series of brilliant victories on the battlefield, the young king led his army deep into the interior of Russia in 1708–9. There he met with a disastrous defeat.

After an extended exile in Turkey, Charles XII again took up arms and was killed in Norway in 1718. Among historians there has been much dispute as to whether the fatal bullet came from the enemy or one of the king's own soldiers.

In any event, his death marked the end of Sweden's Baltic empire. Only Finland and part of Pomerania remained. Furthermore, decades of unremitting warfare left the country weak and in debt.

The Golden Age

The years of peace that followed were a Golden Age of culture and science in Sweden. During this period, Carolus Linnaeus laid the foundations for modern botanical science by classifying the flora of the world; Anders Celsius, the physicist and astronomer, developed the centigrade thermometer with 100 degrees between the freezing and boiling point of water, a scale still used by most countries; and Emanuel Swedenborg anticipated the findings of modern scientific research in a remarkable

The Pacifist Who Invented Dynamite

Alfred Nobel (1833–96), inventor, engineer and industrialist, held more than 350 patents during his lifetime. While still in his teens he became an accomplished linguist—fluent in English, German, French and Russian in addition to his native Swedish—and a first-rate chemist. He was also an avid student of philosophy and English literature.

The paradox is that Nobel, a pacifist at heart, should have invented dynamite, which proved such a boon to modern warfare. He also patented blasting gelatin, a substance more powerful than dynamite, and invented smokeless gunpowder. These products formed the basis of his industrial empire which spread across five continents.

Nobel established the celebrated prizes in his will, drawn up a year before his death. They were to go to those who "shall have conferred the greatest benefit on mankind" with the stipulation that "no consideration whatever shall be given to the nationality of the candidates". His entire fortune, which amounted to many millions of dollars, was used for this purpose.

First awarded in 1901, Nobel prizes fell into five categories: physics, chemistry, medicine or physiology, literature and achievements in the cause of peace—the fields which mirrored Nobel's own interests. He was a scientist who loved literature (Shelley was his favourite) and abhorred war.

number of ways and founded a new church.

Culture flourished during the reign of Gustav III (1771–92). The king, an ardent supporter of music, literature and art, founded the Royal Opera and the Swedish Academy to counter French influence and encourage the Swedish language. (It now awards the Nobel prizes for literature.) He also gave the nation what is known as the elegant "Gusta-vian" style, the local version of Louis XVI style.

But then Gustav III was assassinated at a masked ball in the Stockholm Opera House and Sweden became involved in the Napoleonic wars. In 1809 a new constitution was adopted which gave Swedes many of the rights they enjoy today. About the same time, Finland, which had been a part of Sweden for 600 years, was taken by Russia under an **23** agreement between Czar Alexander I and Napoleon. Soon afterwards, the Bernadotte dynasty was "imported" from France. A field marshal under Napoleon, Jean Baptiste Bernadotte was elected to the Swedish throne (as Karl XIV Johan) in the hope of obtaining French assistance in recovering Finland. The compromise was Denmark's cession of Norway in 1814. It remained attached to Sweden until 1905.

An agricultural crisis hit Sweden towards the end of the 19th century. The hard times led hundreds of thousands of Swedes to emigrate to America in the 1880s. But in many ways far-reaching social and political changes in Sweden made life a lot better for those who stayed home. Among other things, the four-estate parliament was supplanted by a two-house version. (The latest development occurred in 1971, when parliament was reduced to a single house.)

The 20th Century

The 20th century saw Sweden shifting rapidly from a farming to an industrial economy. More and more people moved from rural areas to towns and cities. The emigration to America also continued, and by 1930 about a million Swedes (one out of five) had settled in the New World.

At the same time the power of the labour unions and their ally, the Social Democratic Party, founded in 1889, was increasing. Hjalmar Branting, the great socialist leader, became prime minister in 1920, setting the stage for the vast social reforms that were to make Sweden the world's leading welfare state.

Swedes pay the highest taxes in the world to support cradle to grave security, but most feel they get a lot in return for their money—in the form of housing subsidies, maternity leave for expectant mothers, child allowances, free hospital care, old-age pensions and a host of other benefits. These and other social measures, however, fall far short of outright socialism, and the bulk of Swedish industry is still controlled by private interests.

The solid success of Swedish industry, in fact, has not only made the welfare state possible but also helped to give the Swedes one of the world's highest standards of living. The nation has been able to exploit

Nobel Prize reception is held in the Golden Hall of Stadshuset.

The image of modern Stockholm captured in one enormous glass façade.

effectively its few natural resources, namely iron ore and timber.

The technical genius of the Swedes has played a significant role in building an affluent society, too. Many Swedish companies of international scope have been developed on the basis of Swedish inventions: dynamite (invented by Alfred Nobel), the modern calculator (W.T. Odhner), the self-aligning ball-bearing (Sven Wingquist), automatic beacons and light buoys (Gustaf Dalén), the centrifugal cream separator (Gustaf de Laval), and the three-phase alternating electrical current system (Jonas Wenström).

Innovations in many fields,

Sweden remains a constitutional monarchy with the king as head of state, but actual power rests solely with parliament, one of the oldest legislative bodies in the world. The Social Democrats, in office for a record 44 years before being defeated for a brief spell between 1976 and 1982 by a coalition of non-socialist parties, have been the dominant factor in 20th-century Swedish politics. Nonetheless, the country has generally been governed by consensus, with decisions reached by discreet compromise. All the political parties, including the conservatives, have supported the broad outlines of the welfare state.

Although Sweden fought its last war back in 1814, it was only during this century that the country adopted the policy of strict neutrality that kept it out of both world wars. It has avoided joining military pacts like NATO, and has even chosen to stay out of the Common Market.

from sex education in the schools to urban planning, have resulted in Sweden being looked upon as a kind of "model country". Sociologists, architects, educators and other specialists have come in great numbers to see what they could learn from the Swedish experience. Sweden has also been a pace setter in applied arts, and for many years the expression "Swedish Modern" was virtually a synonym for good design and quality.

But the Swedes are by no means isolationists. The country has been an active and loyal supporter of the United Nations ever since its inception. And Swedes have earned a reputation as defenders of the downtrodden and critics of despotism the world over. **27**

What to See

Look at a map of Stockholm and what do you see? A lot of blue (water) and green (parks), many islands and bridges, and streets that appear to run in all directions without rhyme or reason. You get a bird's-eye view of all this from the observation platform of **Kaknästornet**, the tallest building in Scandinavia. The vista is absolutely stunning, an excellent visual introduction to Stockholm. You'll see at once that the city is beautiful, but it may also strike you as rather confusing.

Actually, getting around Stockholm is not as difficult as you might think. Much of what you'll want to see is concentrated in and around Norrmalm, the city centre, and Gamla Stan, the Old Town. A good public transport system makes the other parts of the city easily accessible too.

As a starter, take a city **boat**

tour from Strömkajen, near the Grand Hotel, or Stadshusbron (City Hall Bridge). The one-hour tour circles the island of Djurgården, Stockholm's biggest park area, while the longer (two-hour) excursion takes in both the Baltic Sea and Lake Mälaren sides of Stockholm. You go under the bridges and through narrow channels and canals, passing dockyards, apartment houses, quayside boulevards, castles and parks. It's great fun, and a fine way to get the feel of the city.

Bus trips include several Grand City tours which cover a big chunk of Stockholm (from Karl XII:s Torg near Operakällaren). Knowledge-able, multi-lingual guides point

The city that floats on water: Stockholm, with its myriad islands, bridges and towers, its abundant greenery and water all, all around.

out and explain the sights on both the bus and boat tours.

Stockholm's trams, an attraction themselves, run from Norrmalmstorg to Waldemarsudde daily in summer (weekends only in winter). The "special" tickets they require can be bought on the tram. A less quaint, but extensive bus and subway system offers cheap one- and three-day tourist tickets. Taxis are very expensive.

Comfortable shoes are a must, for Stockholm is a walker's town, and it best reveals its multiple charms and moods to the casual stroller.

City Centre

You'll undoubtedly be spending a good deal of time in the New Stockholm, in Norrmalm, the city's northern sector. This is where the business, banking, shopping and entertainment facilities are concentrated, as well as the bigger hotels, the main city air terminal and the railway station.

Central Stockholm has been almost entirely rebuilt. A bewildering array of shapes and materials characterizes the soaring towers of the new buildings. Old streets have been replaced by modern shopping

Heart of the new city centre, Sergels Torg with its stunning glass obelisk; Kulturhuset has a busy programme of music and art, fun and games.

malls with new restaurants, cinemas and boutiques.

Your first goal should be **Sergels Torg** (Sergel Square), focal point of the new city centre. When you see a gigantic glass obelisk rising from a fountain in the middle of a busy traffic circle, you'll know you're there. The square's lower-level mall, built as a shopping centre, has become a gathering place for angry people, something like the speak-

er's corner of Hyde Park. Most protest marches start here.

The lower mall also serves as the entry to the glass-fronted **Kulturhuset** (House of Culture), which attracts thousands of visitors daily. They come to see films and videos, to look at art and handicrafts exhibitions, to listen to music, poetry, dramatic readings and debates. Here, too, can be found the Stockholm Stadsteatern (Municipal Theatre), **33** which stages both modern and classical plays in Swedish.

In Kulturhuset's innovative library you can sink down in an easy chair fitted out with earphones and listen to an extensive selection of classical, pop or jazz music on records and tapes. There are private booths for recorded language study, foreign newspapers and periodicals and a special children's corner where the earphones broadcast fairy tales.

A short walk through a shopping mall, usually animated by the music and songs of street performers, brings you to **Hötorget** (Haymarket Square), the northern end of a row of glass skyscrapers that starts at Sergels Torg. Hötorget's open-air market, selling fresh fruit, vegetables and flowers, adds a touch of colour to this square. Also on Hötorget is **Konserthuset** (Concert Hall), a neo-classical building distinguished by an unusual façade of Corinthian pillars and bronze portals. The Stockholm Philharmonic Orchestra plays in this hall, where you can also hear everything from chamber music to pop melodies. In front of the building you'll see Carl Milles' **Orpheus Fountain,** one of the late Swedish sculptor's finest works. (See also p. 55.)

34   Double back to Sergels Torg,

turn left, and you're on **Hamngatan,** one of the main shopping streets. Its tenants include NK (short for Nordiska Kompaniet), Sweden's biggest department store, and newcomers like Gallerian, a covered shopping mall with many stores and restaurants.

Sverigehuset (Sweden House), Hamngatan 27, dispenses information about Sweden. Just inside the entrance is a regional tourist office, which provides information on Stockholm and surrounding areas. You'll also find a bookshop.

Next door, Stockholm's liveliest park, **Kungsträdgården** (Royal Gardens), stretches from Hamngatan down to the waters of Strömmen. Established as a royal pleasure garden in the 16th century for the exclusive use of the court and the aristocracy, Kungsträdgården is now a favourite gathering place for Stockholmers and visitors during the summer months. Refreshment stands, cafés, open-air restaurants, botanical exhibits and statues line the park. There is an outdoor stage

Kungsträdgården, the city's liveliest park, offers entertainment for Stockholmers of all ages.

Finding Your Way

Knowing a few key geographical terms in Swedish may help unravel some of the enigmas of a strange city. Note that the words for street, square and so on are often tacked on to place names, as in Skräddargränd, Tailors' Lane. Here are some of the most common ones you'll come across:

bro	bridge
gata	street
gränd	lane
hamn	port
holme	island
kyrka	church
ö	island
plan, plats	square
sjö	lake
slott	castle
stad	city
torg	square
väg	road

for band, rock, chamber music and choral concerts. You can do just about anything in this park—take a folk dance lesson, watch a marionette show, play ping-pong, badminton or stand-up chess, ice-skate (in winter), stroll under long rows of linden trees or simply relax on a bench and watch the crowd go by.

Continuing east along Hamngatan, you'll pass the **Hallwylska Museet** at No. 4. This patrician mansion, built in the 1890s, contains 70 perfectly preserved rooms crammed with Gobelin tapestries, china figurines, Flemish and Dutch paintings, antique furniture, assorted *objets d'art* and, in the library, a bowling alley. At Nybroplan, there's the **Dramatiska Teatern** (Royal Dramatic Theatre), the place where such notable actors as Greta Garbo, Ingrid Bergman and Max von Sydow began their careers. Before his death in 1953, American playwright Eugene O'Neill bequeathed his last plays to the Dramatic Theatre, and their world premières, including that of *Long Day's Journey into Night*, were staged here. August Strindberg, a native Stockholmer, is frequently and splendidly performed, as are Shakespeare and other classics, and, of course, contemporary playwrights.

From Nybroplan walk along Nybrokajen, a quayside street facing a bay lined with boats. If you continue along the water's edge you'll soon reach **Nationalmuseum** (see pp. 56–57). Now head north, passing the Grand Hotel and the white steamers that go out to the Stockholm archipelago, then turn left at Arsenalsgatan, which cuts through the lower end of Kungsträdgården.

You'll see the statue of King Charles XII, Sweden's most celebrated historical figure, and further along the 17th-century church **Jakobs Kyrka**. Pause a moment here to look at the lovely portals, particularly the one on the southern side which dates from 1644.

Up ahead is Gustav Adolfs Torg, a large square with an equestrian statue of King Gustavus Adolphus, the Swedish hero of the Thirty Years' War. On the east side of the square you'll see **Operan** (the Royal Opera), housed in a rather somber baroque-style building from 1898. King Gustav III, a great patron of the arts, founded the opera in 1773. And it was here (in the original opera house) that he was shot and killed in 1792 at a masked ball. Verdi, incidentally, used this drama as the basis for his opera *The Masked Ball*.

The Royal Opera has a long and distinguished history. Some of the world's greatest singers—from Jenny Lind, the 19th-century "Swedish Nightingale" who made a fabulously successful singing tour in the United States, to Jussi Björling and Birgit Nilsson—have started here. This remarkable institution puts on nearly 400 performances of opera and ballet each season.

Gamla Stan

Stockholm's past is neatly concentrated in Gamla Stan (the Old Town), known as the "city between the bridges". On this small island—actually four islands—in the heart of the city, Stockholm got its start more than 700 years ago. The cobbled lanes and winding alleys of the Old Town follow the original medieval street plan. Its houses, palaces and soaring spires are steeped in history, and you'll get the impression of being transported back several centuries, too.

Exploring Gamla Stan is a must for every visitor to Stockholm. Start from Gustav Adolfs Torg and cross over Strömmen, where the waters of the Baltic Sea and Lake Mälaren meet, on the gracefully arched bridge of Norrbro. On your right you have Riksdagshuset (House of Parliament) and up ahead the massive façade of **Kungliga Slottet** (the Royal Palace), which dominates the northern end of the Old Town.

It *was* known as the biggest palace in the world where royalty lived (600 rooms), but the king and queen have now decided that Drottningholm is more suited to family life. The original Tre Kronor (Three

Crowns) castle on this site burned down in 1697. It wasn't until 1754 that the present building was completed, according to a design by Nicodemus Tessin the Younger, a notable court architect.

Kungliga Slottet is remarkably accessible to the public. Anyone can walk through the inner courtyard, and the main parts of the building are open to visitors. They come to admire the beautifully preserved rococo interior of the Royal Chapel or to look at Queen Kristina's silver throne in the Hall of State. The royal jewels, displayed in the **Treasury**, include the king's crown, first used for Erik XIV's coronation in 1561, and the queen's crown, studded with almost 700 diamonds, designed in 1751 for Queen Lovisa Ulrika.

Among the other palace highlights: **royal apartments** and galleries with magnificent baroque and rococo interiors, containing priceless 17th-cen-

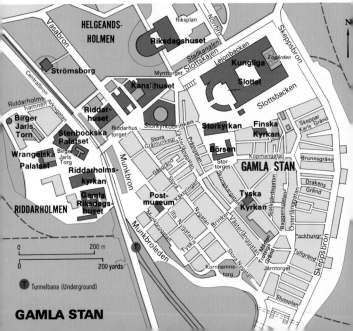

GAMLA STAN

tury Gobelin tapestries, paintings, glass, china, jewellery and furniture collected over the centuries by kings and queens. In addition to the Treasury (Skattkammaren), the palace houses three more museums. The **Palace Museum** in the cellar contains artefacts from the Middle Ages; the **Museum of Antiquities** displays classical sculpture brought from Italy by King Gustav III during the 1780s; and **Livrustkammaren** is the Royal Armoury.

Formerly housed in the Nordic Museum, this is a fascinating collection of the weapons and costumes of Swedish kings. Some of the more unusual exhibits you'll see: the stuffed horse ridden by Gustavus Adolphus when he fell in the Battle of Lützen in 1632, the uniform worn by Charles XII when he was fatally wounded in the trenches near Fredrikshald, Norway, in 1718, and the costume Gustav III had on when he was murdered at the Stockholm Opera Ball, together with the assassin's gun and mask.

The **changing of the guard,**

You can reach out and touch both sides of Mårten Trotzigs Gränd, the narrowest street in Stockholm.

accompanied by music, takes place in the palace's outer courtyard, at 12.15 p.m. on Wednesday and Saturday, every weekday from April to October; at 1.15 p.m. on Sundays all year long.

A gift shop is housed in the palace proper (see p. 83).

The next point of interest in the immediate area is **Storkyrkan** (Great Church), on Slottsbacken, diagonally across from the south façade of the Royal Palace. The city's oldest church (from the 13th century) and the coronation site of most of Sweden's kings, Storkyrkan's dull baroque exterior gives no hint of the beauty of its late-Gothic

church, a most unsavoury event known as the Stockholm Blood Bath took place in 1520. King Christian II of Denmark had some 80 Swedish noblemen beheaded and their heads piled, pyramid-style, in the middle of the square. Among the fine old houses on Stortorget you'll see **Börsen** (the Stock Exchange), a handsome building dating from 1776. The Swedish Academy meets here to elect the Nobel Prize winners in Literature.

What to do now? Actually, the best way to get the feel of the Old Town is to wander about aimlessly. There's something to see or experience at every turn—antique shops housed in 15th- and 16th-century buildings, former merchant palaces, gabled houses with ornate portals, and charming alleyways with quaint names like Gåsgränd (Goose Lane), Drakens Gränd (Dragon Lane), Skeppar Karls Gränd (Skipper Karl's Lane), and so forth. You'll also come across many art shops and galleries, and smart boutiques offering trendy clothes, hand-crafted jewellery, ceramics and

interior. Note, especially, the sculptural ensemble *St. George and the Dragon*, a 15th-century masterpiece executed by Bernt Notke, a woodcarver from Lübeck, which symbolizes Sweden's struggles to break free of Denmark.

In **Stortorget** (Great Square), a few steps from the

41

such. Explore the Old Town haphazardly, by all means, but try to include some of the spots mentioned below in your meandering.

Walk south along **Västerlånggatan**, just west of Stortorget, a long and gently curving medieval shopping street, entirely free of cars. Make a short detour to the left when you reach Tyska Brinken, over to **Tyska Kyrkan** (the German Church). It possesses a fine baroque exterior and an opulent interior from the mid-17th century.

Continue along Västerlånggatan. Near the end you'll find **Mårten Trotzigs Gränd,** the narrowest street in Stockholm. Scarcely more than a yard wide, it's actually a steep, lamp-lit stone stairway leading to Prästgatan.

Västerlånggatan terminates at Järntorget (Iron Market Square) and if you swing around the square you'll be on **Österlånggatan**, a long winding

street dotted with art galleries and craftsmen's shops. Like Västerlånggatan, it runs the length of the island, but it's much more tranquil.

Den Gyldene Freden (The Golden Peace), at Österlånggatan 51, right near Järntorget, is the most famous tavern in the Old Town. Its name comes from the Peace of Nystad of 1721, which marked the end of Charles XII's wars. The historic brick cellar rooms are associated with the 18th-century troubadour Carl Michaël Bellman, a kind of Robert Burns who dropped by here from time to time.

Walking north along Österlånggatan you pass by another St. George and the Dragon statue, and off to your right many picturesque lanes with arched

Stortorget—the city's oldest centre; nearby church of Storkyrkan contains striking 15th-century sculpture, St. George and the Dragon.

entryways that run down to Skeppsbron quay. Österlånggatan takes you back to Slottsbacken and the Royal Palace.

From here, head west on Storkyrkobrinken until you reach a square called Riddarhustorget. This was where the assassin of Gustav III was brutally flogged before being beheaded. On the north side of the square stands the classic 17th-century **Riddarhuset** (House of Nobility), considered by many to be Stockholm's

most beautiful building. The first architect, a Frenchman, was stabbed to death in a dispute over the building plans, but a German, a Dutchman and then the original architect's son, Jean de la Vallée, completed the admirable red-brick and sandstone structure.

Just a stone's throw away, across a bridge, is the tiny island of **Riddarholmen** (Isle of the Nobility), closely linked to the Old Town. A Stockholm landmark dominates the isle—**Riddarholmskyrkan,** unmistakable because of its distinctive cast-iron spire. Founded as an abbey at the end of the 13th century, this church

View of Gamla Stan. To the right, beautiful, classic Riddarhuset and Riddarholmskyrkan's iron spire.

has been the burial place of Swedish kings for some 400 years.

Also on Riddarholmen are a former Riksdag building, various palaces and the copper-topped Birger Jarl's tower, erected, in fact, by Gustav Vasa in the 16th century.

From Riddarholmen quay you get a marvellous **view** of Lake Mälaren, the heights of Söder (the southern part of Stockholm), and Stadshuset on Kungsholmen (see p. 53). This is the best spot, incidentally, to photograph the striking City Hall building that appears to rise straight out of the waters of Lake Mälaren.

Djurgården

It's easy to see why Stockholmers love Djurgården (which means Animal Park). This immense, largely unspoiled island of natural beauty, formerly a royal hunting park, has miles of woodland trails, magnificent oaks (a few go back to Viking times), surprising statuary tucked away in the green, outdoor coffee shops and restaurants, and some of the city's principal museums.

Djurgården is perfect for picnicking, jogging, horseback riding, or enjoying a walk in quiet surroundings. One of the favourite promenades is along a path that winds and dips but never strays too far from the shoreline of Djurgårdsbrunnsviken, a lovely channel that merges with an even lovelier canal. In the winter, when the water freezes over, people walk, skate or ski on the ice.

There are a number of ways to reach the western end of Djurgården, where the island's major attractions are grouped. From Gamla Stan, you can take the ferryboat at the southern end of Skeppsbron quay —a short, delightful trip on a little steamer. From Norrmalmstorg, you can take the tram. From central Stockholm, there's the bus (No. 44 **45** or 47). Or, even better, you can go on foot, starting at Nybroplan and then following **Strandvägen,** a fashionable quayside boulevard in the Östermalm section of town.

This is a very pleasant walk, either along the centre promenade lined with linden trees or the quay, where many old schooners are anchored. Keep on Strandvägen until you reach Djurgårdsbron, the bridge to Djurgården. After crossing it, you'll come to **Nordiska Museet,** a big, multi-towered building on your right (see p. 58). Directly behind it is the **Vasamuseet,** where you'll see the world's oldest identified ship and Stockholm's number one tourist attraction.

This 17th-century man-of-war capsized and sank in the Stockholm harbour, a few hundred feet from the spot where she was launched on her maiden voyage in 1628. And there the *Wasa* remained, forgotten, until 1956 when a marine archaeologist discovered her.

The salvaging of the *Wasa,* an incredible, almost miraculous feat, has added a colourful chapter to the annals of marine history. In addition to the well-preserved, elaborately decorated hull, over 24,000 items from the ship, including hundreds of wooden sculptures, have been recovered by divers who had to sift through some 40,000 cubic yards of mud in the *Wasa's* grave.

In the lengthy restoration, experts were faced with the stupendous task of piecing together 14,000 fragments recovered from the deep. Finally complete, the *Wasa* was moved to her own permanent, spacious quarters on Galärvarvsvägen. In the open-plan museum, visitors can inspect her in her entirety on seven levels. Children will especially enjoy "sailing" the *Wasa* using computer simulators.

There are also exhibition halls nearby, containing ornaments and other objects from the ship—pottery, coins, pewter tankards, glassware, clay pipes, cannon balls and items of clothing taken from the skeletons of 18 *Wasa* seamen found on the ship. Among the oddest discoveries were a box containing butter (rancid, of course) and a flask of rum, still drinkable after more than three centuries.

To best visit the *Wasa,* start by watching the introductory film (shown hourly)

46

A bright medley of red-and-black roofs in Djurgården.

or take a guided tour (several times daily).

Further on, you'll approach the **Biologiska Museet** on your left (see p. 60). Follow Djurgårdsvägen to **Liljevalchs Konsthall** which mounts excellent exhibitions of paintings, sculpture and handicrafts.

Only a few steps away is **Gröna Lund,** or Tivoli, Stockholm's amusement park. It has the usual fun things, like shooting galleries, a merry-go-round, tunnel of love, and so on, but also a first-rate theatre and open-air stage where top Swedish and foreign artists perform.

While you're in this area pause to have a look at the cluster of old houses on some of the narrow streets near the amusement park. This charming little community, called **Djurgårdsstaden,** was founded more than 200 years ago.

Now cross Djurgårdsvägen and you'll be at the entrance to **Skansen,** the world's first and most famous open-air muse-

um, the prototype for all the others that followed. Beautifully situated on a 75-acre hill, it was created by Artur Hazelius in 1891. The idea was to establish a kind of Sweden in miniature, to show how the people—from farmers to aristocrats—lived and worked during different eras.

Some 150 historic buildings from various parts of Sweden form Skansen's core. They represent a bygone way of life, a culture that was fast disappearing after the advent of the Industrial Revolution. Gathered here are reassembled cottages, manor houses, peasant and Lapp huts and ancient

Out of the deep, a macabre wooden sculpture retrieved from the wreck of the warship Wasa that sank in 1628; a quaint house near Gröna Lund.

farmsteads, complete with cows, pigs and other farm animals. Also country stores and city shops, including a bakery and an old pharmacy, and the 18th-century Seglora Kyrka, which is very popular for weddings. Craftsmen ply their trades in old goldsmiths', bookbinders', potters', and glassblowers' workshops. Guided tours leave hourly from Bollnästorget in the summer.

Skansen's zoo features northern animals, such as reindeer, seals, wolves and deer, as well as fauna from other parts of the world. The park has a special children's area, Lill-Skansen, with rabbits, chickens, kittens, guinea pigs and other small animals, not to mention an aquarium, botanical gardens, indoor and outdoor restaurants, public dance floors and an open-air stage. There is always something going on—a concert or jazz session, folk singing and folk dancing, and musical plays.

You can spend a whole day or more at Skansen without getting in the least bored, and the park is also very pleasant in the evening. The night view of Stockholm is particularly lovely from this hilltop—you see the city lights reflected in the water, sparkling in all directions.

Outside Skansen take bus No. 47 to **Waldemarsudde** (only a short ride), on the south shore of Djurgården. This is the former house and art gallery of Prince Eugen, known as Sweden's "Painter Prince". When he died in 1947 at the age of 82, he left his property to the nation. The public can visit both the house and the gallery in their lovely setting of parkland and terraced flower gardens that step down to a channel of the Baltic Sea.

Waldemarsudde has an ambitious collection of Swedish paintings, mostly from the late 19th century. There are also more than a hundred works by Prince Eugen, who was a fine landscape painter as well as an outstanding art collector. The garden contains a number of first-rate sculptures.

A final stop in Djurgården: **Thielska Galleriet,** a gallery with a good collection of French and Scandinavian art. Outstanding are a group of engravings and paintings by the Norwegian Edvard Munch. Also some works by August Strindberg, whose fame as a

There's always something going on at Skansen, the outdoor museum.

dramatist has tended to obscure the fact that he could also paint. The gallery is housed in a Jugendstil house built by a wealthy banker, on the southeast end of the island. If you're energetic, you can walk there from Waldemarsudde. From downtown Stockholm you take bus No. 69 at Norrmalmstorg.

Stadshuset and Other Sights

Most of the major points of interest are found in the areas covered thus far—Stockholm centre, the Old Town and Djurgården. But there are still a number of choice attractions

Artists and craftsmen from all over Sweden contributed to Stadshuset, Stockholm's handsome city hall set on the shore of Lake Mälaren.

left to see. Foremost of these is **Stadshuset** (the City Hall), located on Kungsholmen island west of the city centre. You can get there by crossing Stadshusbron (City Hall Bridge) from Tegelbacken.

When William Butler Yeats came to Stockholm in 1923 to receive the Nobel Prize for Literature, he took a look at the new City Hall and said: "No work comparable in method and achievement has been accomplished since the Italian cities felt the excitement of the Renaissance..."

Yeats was not alone in lavishing praise on Stockholm's City Hall. Designed by Ragnar Östberg, the building rises gracefully and dramatically on the shore of Lake Mälaren. Artists and craftsmen from all over Sweden contributed to its creation, and it has become a fitting symbol, almost an architectural hymn to the city.

Stadshuset is worth several hours of your time, and even then you'll only get an inkling of what went into the construction of this remarkable building. The hand-cut brick façades and square tower capped by three golden crowns, the black granite reliefs, pillars and arches—all miraculously blend together to form a unified and coherent whole, a monumental attempt to fuse together the many different elements that make up Stockholm.

Join one of the guided tours through the City Hall's handsome interior. Highlights include the **Golden Hall**—covered with striking mosaics—the huge glass-domed Blue Hall (which is actually red)—where the Nobel Prize banquets are held—and the Prince's Gallery with murals executed by Prince Eugen.

In the terraced garden by the

water you'll find Carl Eldh's sculptures of the dramatist August Strindberg, the poet Gustaf Fröding and the painter Ernst Josephson. Also here, on top of a 45-foot column, is Christian Eriksson's bronze statue of Engelbrekt, Sweden's great hero of the Middle Ages.

For a superb **view** of the Old Town and the central parts of Stockholm, go up to the top of the City Hall Tower.

Extending west of Stadshuset is **Norr Mälarstrand,** a landscaped promenade that follows the water's edge all the way to the big Västerbron (Western Bridge). It's invariably crowded with strolling Stockholmers and parents pushing baby carriages, espe-

Overlooking an inlet of the Baltic, beautiful sculptures in a beautiful setting: Millesgården, home, studio and garden of Carl Milles.

cially on a sunny Sunday afternoon. You may want to join them on this pleasant walk.

Whatever you do, don't miss **Millesgården,** the home, studio and garden of the late Carl Milles, Sweden's famous modern sculptor. Although Milles lived and worked abroad for long periods, mostly in the United States, he was extremely fond of his place on the island suburb of Lidingö and managed to spend most of his summers here.

The beautifully terraced gardens overlooking an inlet of the Baltic provide a superb setting for replicas of Milles' best work. Included here are some of his most popular pieces— *Man and Pegasus, Europa and the Bull* and the spectacular *Hand of God.* There is also an important collection of Greek and Roman sculpture, and the work of other sculptors.

Millesgården itself is a work of art, the creation of a man who worshipped beauty. Silver birch and pine trees mingle naturally with statues and fountains, rose beds and urns of flowers blend with marble columns and flights of limestone steps. Carl Milles died in 1955, at the age of 80, and both he and his wife are buried in a small chapel in the garden. Take the underground from Ropsten to Torsvik, or bus No. 201, 202, 204, 205, 206 or 212.

If you have the time, go over to **Söder,** the large island on Stockholm's south side, with steep cliffs plunging down into the Baltic and Lake Mälaren. It's a place with a very special atmosphere, quite different from the other parts of the city. Söder contains a number of small, closely integrated neighbourhoods, clusters of rust-red wooden cottages and artist studios in rural-like settings.

Start at Slussen, a cloverleafed traffic circle above the narrow canal connecting the lake with the sea. In the summer you'll see many pleasure boats lined up here, waiting for the canal lock to be opened.

Slussen is the site of **Stadsmuseum,** the Stockholm City Museum (see p. 61), and one of the city's most curious sights: **Katarinahissen,** a lift that rises in an open shaft to the roof of a tall building. From the top you'll get a classic view of the Old Town. A gangway takes you over to a clifftop neighbourhood of old houses with hidden courtyards.

Now head for **Fjällgatan,** east of the Katarina district, where most of the city sightseeing buses stop. This little street, perched along the edge of a **55** towering ridge overlooking the Baltic, affords one of the very best panoramas of Stockholm. Not far from here is a charming colony of shuttered, fenced-in cottages grouped on the slopes of a grassy hill around the Sofia Kyrka.

You'll see more picturesque houses at Mariaberget, a hill west of Slussen. And from the heights of **Skinnarviksberget,** still another stunning view of Stockholm encompassing Lake Mälaren and Stadshuset.

Old Masters hang in National-museum; whimsical Picasso figures lounge outside Moderna Museet.

Museums

A number of important museums, such as Skansen, the Warship Wasa and Millesgården, have already been covered. Here is a description of other major museums in Stockholm, plus some of specialized interest.

First Five

Nationalmuseum (National Museum of Fine Arts). One of the oldest museums in the world—opened to the public in 1794—it first occupied a wing of the Royal Palace. The museum moved to its present site,

an Italian Renaissance-style building, in 1866.

The collection is impressive and not only because of its size. Among the old masters, you'll find ten Rembrandts, plus important works by Rubens, El Greco and Brueghel and a choice group of Chardin oils. Courbet, Cézanne, Gauguin, Renoir and Manet are represented, as well as Swedish artists such as Carl Larsson, Bruno Liljefors (known for his vivid nature studies) and Anders Zorn. The latter's *Midsummer Dance* is a wonderful evocation of Midsummer's Eve in the province of Dalarna. Also look for François Bouch-er's *The Triumph of Venus*, considered his greatest work, and *The Lady and the Veil* by Alexander Roslin (1718–93), an excellent Swedish painter.

In addition, the collections include thousands of prints, engravings and miniatures, more than 200 Russian icons and a selection of handicrafts.

Moderna Museet (Museum of Modern Art). With op, pop and all kinds of "happenings", this stimulating, trend-setting institution has kept up with the best of contemporary art from the rest of Europe and the United States. The museum's extensive collection of 20th-

century art includes Matisse, Braque, Léger, Modigliani, Klee and Rauschenberg, plus top Swedish artists like Isaac Grünewald and Bror Hjorth.

Some of the acquisitions have been gifts from prominent artists. One, a bizarre sculptural group by Jean Tinguely and Niki de Saint Phalle, is called *The Paradise*. Each day, when the current is turned on, Tinguely's aggressive masculine machines attack Miss Phalle's gigantic women.

The museum also offers music, film and theatre programmes, as well as changing exhibitions in its fine **Museum of Photography** in the building's western gallery.

Östasiatiska Museet (Museum of Far Eastern Antiquities). This enormous collection covers art from Japan, Korea, India and China, from the Stone Age to the 19th century. The museum's collection of ancient Chinese art, considered the best in the world outside of China, includes 1,800 objects bequeathed to the museum by the late King Gustaf Adolf VI, a distinguished archaeologist and collector and a respected authority on Chinese art.

Other highlights: Stone Age pottery from about 2,000 B.C.; a reconstructed Chinese grave, with urns and axe heads grouped around a skeleton; colourful ceramics from the Ming Dynasty (1368–1644), and a series of superb bronze sacrificial vessels.

Nordiska Museet (Nordic Museum). Artur Hazelius, the creator of Skansen, founded this museum which illustrates life in Sweden from the 16th century to the present. As you enter the building you're greeted by Carl Milles' enormous oak statue of Gustav Vasa, father of modern Sweden.

There is a lot to look at here—more than one million objects, in fact. You'll see exhibits depicting the history of upper class fashions, a very interesting section on food and drink with table settings from different periods and a gallery of Swedish peasant costumes from the first part of the 19th century. Also on view, interesting exhibits on the nomadic Lapps and their reindeer, and a section devoted to Nordic folk art that includes Swedish wall paintings, Norwegian tapestries, Finnish drinking vessels and Danish embroidery.

Family life was a favourite theme of Swedish painter Carl Larsson.

Historiska Museet (Museum of National Antiquities). Ten thousand years of history are eloquently unfolded in this excellent museum. Before going inside have a good look at the main entrance. The "door of history" there, covered with a multitude of allegorical and historical figures in bronze relief, is the work of Swedish sculptor Bror Marklund.

The museum has more than 30 rooms, so it's best to pick up a floor plan, available with explanations in English. The ground floor exhibits start with artefacts fashioned by the earliest inhabitants of Sweden, during the Mesolithic and Neolithic periods. The Viking Age has yielded a rich collection of gold and silver objects, fine examples of ornamental art, weapons, rune stones from the isle of Gotland. And from an earlier epoch, see the Treasure of Vendel, a remarkable burial site with the dead in their boats surrounded by every-day objects.

Magnificent examples of medieval church art can be seen on the first floor. There are wooden crucifixes modelled after Byzantine art, beautifully painted and sculptured altar pieces, baptismal fonts, textile wall hangings, gold chalices and processional crosses. One

room consists of a reconstruction of a typical medieval country church.

The second floor houses the **Kungliga Myntkabinettet** (Royal Coin Cabinet), with fascinating specimens of international medallic art from the 15th century to the present, and about 400,000 coins from all over the world, going back to 650 B.C.

Other Museums of Interest

Armémuseum (Army Museum) contains weapons, uniforms, battle trophies and so on, from the 16th century to the present. The collections include everything from small side arms and artillery to musical instruments of pipers and drummers. This museum underscores the fact that peace-loving Sweden was once a military terror on the continent.

Biologiska Museet (Natural History Museum). Created in 1893 by two very talented men, taxidermist Gustaf Kolthoff and painter Bruno Liljefors, this admirable institution is said to have served as a model for New York's Museum of Natural History.

You can admire 300 different species of Nordic animals and birds, including polar

bears, seals, Arctic wolves, mountain hares and moose, hawk owls, white-tailed eagles, herring gulls, spotted woodpeckers and guillemots nesting on cliffs. They are stuffed, of course, but look eerily real in these ingeniously arranged settings. An absorbing museum for both children and adults.

Medeltidsmuseet (Museum of Medieval Stockholm). Stockholm's newest museum sensation lies beneath the courtyard of the House of Parliament. On view *in situ* are remnants of 13th-century fortifications and a section of the 16th-century town wall, uncovered by con-

struction workers excavating for an underground car park.

Palatial Nordiska Museet shows many aspects of Swedish life.

Postmuseum (Postal Museum) illustrates the history of mail service in Sweden from olden times to the present. The museum has an excellent philatelic department, one of the largest stamp collections for public viewing in the world. Rarities include the first English stamp cancelled on the day of issue, May 6, 1840.

Sjöhistoriska Museet (National Maritime Museum). In a fine building designed by Ragnar Östberg, architect of the City Hall, the museum traces the history of the Swedish navy and merchant marine. Centrepiece of the collection is the stern of the schooner *Amphion*, which won a key naval battle against the Russians in 1790 under Gustav III.

Stockholms Stadsmuseum (Stockholm City Museum), covering the history of Stockholm, is housed appropriately in the former 17th-century town hall. The exhibits include archaeological finds from the area, a fine model of the old **61**

Tre Kronor castle, paintings of the city by various artists, sculptures from the façades of demolished buildings, and all kinds of objects used in the everyday life of the city. You can have coffee and snacks in the museum's charming 19th-century café, and, for children, there is a special corner for play or creative activities.

Strindbergsmuseet (Strindberg Museum) honours August Strindberg, Sweden's most famous playwright. The apartment where he lived during the last years of his life (he died in 1912) has been reconstructed with authentic furnishings, including his writing desk. Three adjoining rooms are devoted to his manuscripts, letters, photos of various actors and actresses who appeared in his plays, etc.

Tekniska Museet (National Museum of Science and Technology). Fathers and sons, and even other members of the family, will be delighted with the exhibits in this well-run museum concerned with Swedish science and technology through the ages. One of the big attractions is a reconstructed iron ore mine in the basement of the building. Another highlight is the Royal Model Chamber, displaying the inventions of Christopher Polhem (1661-1751), a genius known as the "Father of Swedish Technology".

Museum Particulars
The major museums are listed below. Hours may vary, so check beforehand.

Armémuseum, Riddargatan 13. Underground to Östermalmstorg. Open daily 11 a.m.-4 p.m.

Biologiska Museet, Djurgården. Bus No. 44 or 47. Open April to September from 10 a.m. to 4 p.m., October tö March till 3 p.m.

Historiska Museet, Narvavägen 13-17. Underground to Karlaplan or bus 44, 47 or 69. Open Tuesday to Sunday, noon to 5 p.m. Occasional exhibitions also Wednesday till 9 p.m.

Moderna Museet, Skeppsholmen. Buses, same as Nationalmuseum, then on foot to the island of Skeppsholmen. Open 11 a.m. to 9 p.m. Tuesday and Thursday, till 5 p.m. Wednesday, Friday to Sunday, closed on Monday.

Nationalmuseum, Södra Blasieholmen. Bus No. 43, 46, 55 or 62 to Karl XII:s Torg. Open 10 a.m. to 4 p.m., till 9 p.m. on Tuesday, closed on Monday.

Nordiska Museet, Djurgården. Bus No. 44 or 47.

Open from 10 a.m. to 4 p.m., Monday to Friday. Noon to 5 p.m. on weekends.

Östasiatiska Museet, Skeppsholmen. Transport same as Nationalmuseum. Open Wednesday to Sunday, noon to 4 p.m., Tuesday, noon to 9 p.m. Closed on Monday.

Postmuseum, Lilla Nygatan 6, in the Old Town. Bus 48 or 53 or underground to Gamla Stan. Open Monday to Saturday from noon to 3 p.m.; Sunday, 12 to 4 p.m. and, in winter, Thursday 7 to 9 p.m.

Sjöhistoriska Museet, Djurgårdsbrunnsvägen. Bus No. 69 from Norrmalmstorg. Daily from 10 a.m. to 5 p.m. and, in winter, Tuesday evening from 6 to 8.30.

Stockholms Stadsmuseum, Slussen. Underground to Slussen or bus 43, 46, 48, 53, 55 or 59. Open Tuesday to Thursday, 11 a.m. to 7 p.m., Friday to Monday, 11 a.m. to 5 p.m.

Strindbergsmuseet, Drottninggatan 85. Underground to Rådmansgatan. Tuesday to Saturday, 10 a.m. to 4 p.m.; Tuesday, also 7 to 9 p.m.; Sunday, noon to 5 p.m. Closed on Monday.

Tekniska Museet, Museivägen 7. Bus No. 69 from Norrmalmstorg. Open Monday to Friday, 10 a.m. to 4 p.m.; weekends noon to 4 p.m.

Excursions

Stockholm's surroundings more than match the beauty of the city itself. To the east are the islands of the archipelago, and to the west Lake Mälaren with a choice collection of castles and towns at the water's edge. The province of Södermanland, dotted with small lakes, churches and mansions, runs off from Stockholm's southern edge. And to the north is Uppland, a province of prime historical interest, with hundreds of rune stones from the Viking Age.

There are loads of boat excursions all summer long, on graceful old steamers or modern, and faster, motor launches. Most of those heading for the Baltic islands leave from either Strömkajen or Norra Blasieholmshamnen, both near the Grand Hotel. Stadshusbron, next to the City Hall, is the departure point for boats around Lake Mälaren.

You can also choose from a variety of bus tours, train excursions and some package trips that include an overnight stay in a hotel. The Stockholm Information Service can give you the details (see p. 124). **63**

⚓ Stockholm Archipelago

The Swedes call the Stockholm archipelago Skärgården, which means "garden of skerries". It's a good description. Huge and infinitely varied, this garden consists of some 24,000 rocky islands of all shapes and sizes, extending for 30 miles into the Baltic. There is nothing quite like it anywhere else in the world.

In its day the archipelago served as a place of refuge for pirates and smugglers. Later, fishermen lived in unpainted wooden shacks on many of the islands, and rich noblemen built great estates.

During this century the archipelago has been the favourite playground of Stockholmers who go out to their summer houses on weekends or for longer vacations. They sail and fish, swim and sun themselves on the smooth boulders.

The archipelago is divided into three distinct sections, each with its own special character and atmosphere. The inner group is made up of larger islands covered with forests and farmland. The middle archipelago consists of a jumble of both large and small islands, some with woods and fields of wildflowers, separated by a labyrinth of narrow channels and sounds. The outer archipelago, mostly uninhabited, is a barren seascape of desolate rock islands.

Here are some of the principal destinations:

Less than an hour away by boat, **Vaxholm** is an attractive waterfront town in the inner archipelago. Its chief attraction is the 16th-century **Vaxholm fortress,** which used to guard the straits here and is now a museum. Open afternoons in summer.

Also worth visiting is the old homestead museum Norrhamnen. It is housed in two old buildings, the former homes of fishing families. Vaxholm has many waterside strolling paths, and from the harbour you get a day-long view of motorboats and sailboats trooping through the narrow channel as they head for more distant points in the archipelago.

Three and one-half hours away by steamer—with a restaurant on board—or two hours by motor launch, **Sandhamn** is located on a Baltic island at the outer edge of the archipelago. This fairly long trip has the advantage of taking in all the diverse and

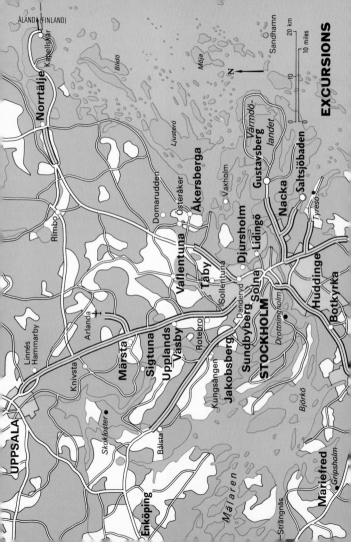

dramatic elements that make up this island world.

An important pilot station since the end of the 17th century, Sandhamn is a yachting centre and home of the fashionable Royal Swedish Yacht Club. The tiny, charming village has only about 100 year-round residents. But the figure swells in the summer when tourists and Stockholmers who have summer cottages there invade the island. Sandhamn's summer amenities include several hotels, an old inn, a restaurant with dancing and good swimming and sailing facilities. In July the island plays host to an international regatta.

Less than 30 minutes by train from Slussen, **Saltsjöbaden** is a posh suburb and resort area in a lovely setting at the edge of the archipelago. Much of the activity here is centred around the Grand Hotel Saltsjöbaden, where you can eat and drink. Outdoor activities include swimming, sailing, tennis, riding and golf.

The splendid **Tyresö Castle,** 45 minutes by bus from Skanstull, sits on an inlet southeast of the city. This 17th-century country estate once belonged to Gabriel Oxenstierna, one of Sweden's leading noblemen. Now a museum open to the public, its collections include interesting period furniture and paintings.

One more suggestion—why not have a look at another country. You can do this by cruising to **Mariehamn,** capital of the Åland islands—3,850 square miles of bays, inlets, islands and skerries—about midway between Sweden and Finland. This autonomous predominantly Swedish-speaking province of Finland has a population of 20,000.

The day cruises leave in the morning, stop for a couple of hours in Mariehamn, and are back in Stockholm by late evening. You can also take a 24-hour excursion, sleeping on board in a comfortable cabin, or you can spend the night in a hotel in Mariehamn. The town has good accommodation and a number of excellent restaurants.

All these cruise ships, we should add, feature a sumptuous *smörgåsbord,* and the bars, dancing lounges and

Boating is a major summer pastime in and around Stockholm. It's also the best way to explore some of the islands of the archipelago.

nightclubs on board are always lively. Tax-free prices make drinks on these cruises very inexpensive, and since the ships pass through the Stockholm archipelago it's a scenic treat as well.

Lake Mälaren

Mälaren, Sweden's third largest lake, stretches out for more than 70 miles west of the city. This area—the Lake Mälaren Valley—has been justly called the cradle of Swedish civilization. Its most important historic sights are within relatively easy striking distance of Stockholm by road, rail or water.

As a starter, consider a trip to **Björkö** (Birch Island), one of the lake's 300 islands. This was the site of Birka, Sweden's oldest trading centre, where St. Ansgar preached to the heathen in the year 830 and built a church. Obliterated in the 11th century, all that remains of the once flourishing town of Birka are the faint traces of old fortifications and something like 3,000 Viking graves. The island is a pleasant, relaxing place to spend part of a day. You can reach Björkö by boat in two hours, summer only.

One of the most pleasant,

not-to-be-missed excursions is to **Drottningholm Palace,** on a small island in an inlet of Lake Mälaren. A boat trip through a beautiful stretch of Mälaren gets you there in under an hour, or you can take the underground to Brommaplan and change to a bus marked "Mälarö".

This French-style palace, now home of the royal family, is referred to as the Versailles of Sweden and was built in the late 17th century. Its formal

gardens are big and impressive, with statuary, fountains, trees and lawns. Sections of the palace's well-preserved interior—richly decorated with fine tapestries and other works of art—are open to the public.

Open daily May–August from 11 a.m. to 4.30 p.m. (from noon on Sunday), in September from 1 to 3.30 p.m.

Be sure to have a look at the **Chinese Pavilion** *(Kina Slott)*, an unusual combination of rococo and Chinese styles. It was

Gripsholm Castle, built in the 16th century by Gustav Vasa, is a prime attraction on Lake Mälaren.

built on the palace grounds in the 1760s as a gift to Queen Lovisa Ulrika.

Best of all is the **Drottningholm Court Theatre,** adjacent to the palace, one of the world's most famous theatrical establishments. This fully restored 18th-century theatre is unique in that its original sets **69**

(30 in all), stage machinery and props are in perfect working order and still in use. Except for the lighting—electricity has replaced candlelight—nothing has changed since King Gustav III, the patron-of-the-arts, attended opera performances here.

During the summer months operas by Handel, Gluck, Mozart and others, as well as ballet, are performed in this gem of a theatre. Appropriately, the musicians are dressed in authentic period costumes and wear powdered wigs. You may feel that you're attending a court entertainment some 200 years ago.

Before or after the performance, you can have a look at the collections of pictures and costumes tracing the history of stage art. Exhibited in the rooms around the auditorium, they include rare Italian and French theatrical designs from the 16th to the 18th centuries and original sketches by Gustav III's stage painter.

Plan a full day's excursion to **Gripsholm Castle,** another of Lake Mälaren's outstanding attractions. You can get there in an hour and a half by train to LÄGGESTA, and then a short bus ride. The alternative route, by boat, takes three and a half hours, but it is time well spent.

The trip on the *S/S Mariefred,* a coal-fired steamer that has been plying the same route since 1903, is really memorable. You can enjoy a good dinner on board.

At the journey's end you'll see Gripsholm's massive, turreted bulk mirrored like a stage set in the waters of the lake. There was a castle on this site in the 1300s, but the present structure was built by Gustav Vasa' in the 16th century—and subsequently added on to and modified by just about every succeeding Swedish monarch. The castle served as a state prison at one time, and it was in its tower that the deposed King Erik XIV was held captive.

Now a museum, Gripsholm houses one of the largest collections of historical portraits in the world. Don't miss the small castle theatre, built by Gustav III (who was responsible for the Drottningholm Theatre), or the two 16th-century bronze cannons in the outer courtyard, captured during wars with the Russians.

The castle is open daily 10 a.m. to 4 p.m., May to August, except on Whitsun and Midsummer Day. Check with the Stockholm tourist office for times during the rest of the year.

Next door to the castle is

Mariefred, where the steamer to Gripsholm docks. You'll want to pause a while in this attractive little town of yellow and red frame houses, with lovely gardens lined up in tight rows along narrow streets and a cobblestone square. High points are a white baroque church and an 18th-century town hall.

You shouldn't leave Mariefred without taking a ride on the **Östra Södermanlands Järnväg** (East Södermanland Railway), a rolling museum of vintage coaches pulled by an old steam engine. This narrow gauge railway, dating from 1895 and maintained by a group of local rail buffs, runs from Mariefred to Läggesta, a distance of 2½ miles, at a top speed of 7 miles an hour. It's a slow but delightful trip.

Buy your tickets here for a nostalgic ride on Mariefred's 2½-mile, narrow-gauge steam railway.

North to Uppsala

There are three noteworthy destinations on the north shore of Lake Mälaren in the province of Uppland: Sigtuna, Skokloster Castle and Uppsala, linked to the lake by a short canal. All three can be reached easily from Stockholm by train, bus or by boat.

Closest to Stockholm is **Sigtuna,** situated on a beautiful, slender arm of the lake. You can drive there in about 45 minutes, or take a train from Centralstationen and change to a bus at MÄRSTA.

Sigtuna, probably Sweden's oldest town, was founded at the beginning of the 11th century by Olof Skötkonung, the coun-

Sigtuna, one of Sweden's oldest towns, was an early Christian centre.

try's first Christian king. It served as the religious centre of the country—a role later taken over by Uppsala—and has some of the oldest churches. It was also Sweden's first capital and a lively trading port until a series of disasters struck. Estonian pirates raided Sigtuna and burned it to the ground. The town gradually recovered, but Gustav Vasa, fired by the ideas of the Reformation, closed its monasteries. The monks left and the town fell into obscurity.

Today Sigtuna is a lakeside idyll with the ruins of four churches, built between 1060 and 1130. Mariakyrkan (St. Mary's), a 13th-century monastery church, remains as mute testimony to its past glory. Walk along Storgatan, said to be the oldest street in Sweden, and have a look at the quaint, toy-like town hall, dating from 1744. Other points of interest, aside from the church ruins and scattered rune stones from the Viking era, are the Fornhemmet museum, containing local archaeological finds, and the Lundström House, a good example of late 19th-century architecture with furniture from the same period.

The Sigtuna Foundation, an important religious institution, has injected new life into the town. It has played host to many prominent authors and scholars who have come here to put the finishing touches on a book or dissertation in guest rooms facing a cloister and rose garden.

The second goal along this route is **Skokloster,** a magnificent baroque palace on the edge of a lovely bay of Lake Mälaren, about midway between Sigtuna and Uppsala. It was built by Carl Gustaf Wrangel, a field marshal under Gustavus Adolphus in the Thirty Years' War.

The castle's 100 over-sized rooms house a fabulous collection of historical treasures, mostly from the 17th century when Sweden was the pre-eminent European military power. There are tapestries, baroque furniture, silver and glass objects, more than 1,000 paintings and 20,000 rare books and manuscripts, much of it war booty. The arms collection, one of the largest in the world, starts off with crossbows and includes such oddities as a set of gruesome executioner's swords and an 8-foot-long rifle that belonged to Queen Kristina.

From May to September, there are daily guided tours through the castle from 11 a.m. to 4 p.m.

Skokloster's vast estate also has a restaurant, a modern hotel and **Motor Museum,** with a fine collection of vintage and veteran cars and engines. The prize exhibits are an 1899 Renault, an elegant, maroon-coloured 1911 Austin, and a Spitfire engine from the time of the Battle of Britain.

The Motor Museum is open daily from 11 a.m. to 4 p.m. all year round.

History jostles you at virtually every corner in **Uppsala,** an ancient centre of culture, religion and education. It's the seat of the Archbishop of the Swedish Church and home of Uppsala University, one of the

world's great institutions of higher learning, which celebrated its 500th anniversary in 1977. The city (with a population of 150,000) lies 73 kilometres north of Stockholm and can be reached in an hour by train from the Centralstationen.

A quick, free-hand sketch of Uppsala would show the river Fyrisån winding its way through the centre of town, green patina forming on the campus statues, rare and beautiful flowers blooming in the Linnaeus Gardens and old wooden buildings aging gracefully—in sharp contrast to the new glass and steel structures. Above all, Uppsala has a most distinctive silhouette: the twin spires of the cathedral and the round towers of the castle, both centuries-old landmarks, soar over the city.

Begin your sightseeing at **Uppsala Domkyrka** right in the middle of the university grounds. This massive, 13th-century cathedral with 400-foot-high spires required 150 years to complete. Many famous Swedes are buried here: King Gustav Vasa (and his three wives); the remains of

Graceful twin-spires of Uppsala's cathedral dominate university town.

St. Erik, Sweden's patron saint and king who died a martyr in Uppsala in 1160; Emanuel Swedenborg, mystic, scientist and philosopher; and Carl Linnaeus, the botanist—both from Uppsala University. In addition to the tombs, the huge interior contains religious tapestries, articles of silver and gold and many other objects of historical and aesthetic interest.

Pause to look at the medieval wall paintings in the nearby **Trinity Church** (*Helga Trefaldighetskyrkan*) before heading for the **Uppsala Slott** (castle), the cathedral's secular rival. This looming red structure, set on a hill overlooking the town, was begun in the 1540s by Gustav Vasa. Having severed ties with the pope, the king intended the castle to be a symbol of royal power. The cannon were therefore aimed directly at the archbishop's residence.

The castle has been the scene of lavish coronation feasts and many dramatic historical events. It was here, for instance, that Gustavus Adolphus held talks that led Sweden into the Thirty Years' War, and that Queen Kristina gave up her crown (in 1654) before setting off for Rome.

Uppsala Castle now serves as the residence of the provincial governor and is used for civic celebrations. Incidentally, the late Secretary General of the United Nations, Dag Hammarskjöld, grew up in the castle while his father was governor.

Of the university buildings, the most outstanding is **Carolina Rediviva,** which now houses the biggest and oldest library in Sweden, originally founded by Gustavus Adolphus. The collection includes more than two million books and a half million manuscripts and documents, many of medieval origin. Among these are a number of extremely rare items, notably, the **Codex Argenteus** (Gothic Silver Bible), written in the 6th century in silver letters and gold capitals on purple parchment.

Drop into the **Gustavianum,** a university building topped by a most curious room. It's an octagonal anatomical theatre under a striking dome constructed in 1662 by Olof Rudbeck, one of many brilliant scientists who taught and did research at Uppsala University. He used the room to dissect bodies for medical instruction. The Gustavianum also houses the collections of the Victoria Museum of Egyptology.

There are many people who **76** travel to Uppsala with a single

purpose in mind—to visit places connected with Carl Linnaeus, known throughout the world as the "Father of Modern Botany" and the "Flower King". He came to Uppsala in 1728 as a medical student, was appointed lecturer in botany after only two years at the university and became a professor in medicine in 1741. In his lifetime Linnaeus named and described some 10,000 different species of plants.

You can see some of these in the university's **Linnéträdgården** (Svartbäcksgatan 27), containing 1,300 plants arranged according to species exactly as they were in Linnaeus' era. His home in the gardens is now a museum open to the public.

During the summer months botanists lead groups of visitors on walks along three marked trails, following the footsteps of Linnaeus in the forests around Uppsala. You can also take a guided tour to **Hammarby,** Linnaeus' summer home (13 km. from Uppsala), where he received hundreds of students from all over the world. The garden there is said to contain some specimens planted by

Uppsala Slott has been the scene of many dramatic historical events.

Linnaeus himself. The walks and visits to Hammarby are arranged by the Uppsala Tourist Information Centre (in Stadshuset).

You should definitely make an excursion to **Gamla Uppsala** (Old Uppsala), about 3 kilometres out of town, reached by regular bus service from the city centre. This is the site of the ruins of a pagan temple and three huge burial mounds said to contain the remains of kings mentioned in *Beowulf*.

The graves, dating from the 6th century, are called Kungshögarna (Kings' Hills).

A medieval parish church stands solidly on the remnants of the heathen temple where blood flowed freely when human and animal sacrifices were offered up to the gods. Nearby is Disagården, an interesting open-air museum, and the Odinsburg Inn, where you can drink mead *(mjöd)* from old Viking ox-horns.

While Uppsala is a fairly tranquil place most of the year, pent-up emotions virtually explode on Walpurgis Night, traditionally a half-pagan, half-Christian celebration held on

The plants in Linnéträdgården are arranged according to species, as they were in the time of Linnaeus.

the last day of April. The ceremony begins in the afternoon when the undergraduates and friends gather in front of the Carolina Rediviva and, at a signal from the rector of the university, let up a great cheer and put on their white student caps. During the evening, students, professors and alumni march with flaming torches and flags of the "nations" (student clubs representing different Swedish provinces) to the top of the castle hill. Here they sing songs hailing the country and the arrival of spring. The festivities continue at the student clubs until the early hours of morning.

What to Do

Shopping

Shopping in Stockholm is a delightful experience, an entry into a very special and wonderful world of design. The best-known products are those of industrial arts and handicrafts, namely glassware, ceramics, silver, stainless cutlery, textiles and furniture. Sweden's fine reputation in these fields rests solidly on an old tradition of skilled craftsmanship handed down from generation to generation. Contemporary Swedish design, in fact, has its roots in the peasant art of the past.

For most visitors shopping means finding some small Swedish items to take home as personal souvenirs and as gifts for all those expectant friends and relatives. And, usually, these items should also be light-weight and relatively inexpensive. Filling this bill poses a real challenge, but you will almost surely enjoy the search in Stockholm's many beautiful shops and department stores (where English is widely spoken).

Shopping Hours
Most shops open from 9 a.m. to 6 p.m. on weekdays, but on **79**

Saturday usually close early, 1 to 4 p.m. In the winter, department stores stay open later on certain days and, occasionally, open on Sundays.

Value-Added Tax Refunds

VAT, or sales tax, called "Moms" in Sweden, is around 18 per cent on all products and services. This tax is refunded in cash within seven days of purchase at any point of departure to visitors who buy in shops displaying the blue-and-yellow "Tax-Free Shopping" sticker (present your passport). You simply hand over the Tax-free Shopping Cheque provided by the shop (make sure you fill out the back) at the Tax-Free Service counter at ports, airports and aboard ships (non-Scandinavian residents only).

Where to Shop

There are three large department stores in the city centre. PUB, on Hötorget, is right across from the blue Konserthuset. The lively open-air market here makes this as good a place as any to start a circular shopping tour of Stockholm.

From PUB work your way south on Drottninggatan to Åhléns department store and Sergels Torg. An underground

shopping mall here brings you directly to the basement level of NK, Stockholm's classic department store. Moving east from NK along Hamngatan, you come to Norrmalmstorg and Biblioteksgatan, a short, car-free street which takes you to Stureplan. Then head west along broad Kungsgatan and you're soon back to the starting point.

For fun shopping in a marvellous medieval milieu, go to Gamla Stan. Västerlång-

A joy for shoppers and strollers: the medieval streets of Gamla Stan.

gatan, the main pedestrian street bisecting the island, is lined with shops and restaurants. You'll also find interesting boutiques, handicraft workshops, art galleries and antique shops tucked away in the narrow lanes and alleys leading off Västerlånggatan.

Take a look too, at the gift shop in the Royal Palace, with its array of unusual souvenirs.

What to Buy

Glassware. This is, without doubt, Sweden's most famous design product—and one of your best buys. Names like Orrefors, Kosta and Boda are well-known all over the world, and the talented artists and artisans working for these and other glassworks ensure that their reputation for creative design and quality will live on. **81**

Ceramics. Rörstrand and Gustavsberg are the dominant names in this field, but there are many smaller companies. Here again, there is a wide choice: from charming and fanciful items that easily fit your suitcase and wallet to one-of-a-kind sculptures with a price tag to match their considerable size.

Home Furnishings. Swedes have a deep—almost fanatical—fondness for the home and its furnishings, and this is reflected in the great care that goes into the production of furniture. The modern classics of masters like Bruno Mathsson and Carl Malmsten are largely responsible for the many laurels Sweden has gained in this field, but the tradition of good-looking, functional furniture is carried on by younger craftsmen. Textiles, lamps, and kitchen items like wooden salad bowls are also worth looking at.

Stainless Flatware. This is

another superb Swedish product that has justifiably won international recognition. Something practical, as well as beautiful, to take home.

Souvenirs. The brightly painted, hand-carved Dala horse is probably the most typical Swedish souvenir and certainly the most popular. Among other worthwhile items are hand-painted linen tapestries and lovely handmade dolls.

The gift shop in the Royal Palace sells a selection of items copied from pieces on display in Sweden's palaces (replicas of brass candlesticks, glassware, pewter objects, etc.). Other articles, from foodstuffs and place mats to carrier bags, simply bear the royal insignia.

Lapp Handicrafts. Though Stockholm is far from Lapland (which extends beyond the Arctic Circle), many shops stock buckles, knife-handles, pouches and other handcrafted Lapp items made from reindeer antlers and skin.

Furs. In Sweden furs are considered a necessity rather than a luxury because of the cold winters. Look for the Saga label, the mink world's mark of quality and an outstanding product common to all of the Nordic countries.

Suède. Coats, jackets and skirts in suède are excellent buys. Suède, in fact, is a Swedish invention and the French word for Sweden.

Silver. Silversmiths like Sigurd Persson have turned out bold, innovative necklaces, bracelets and rings. They have also fashioned stunning silver bowls, cigarette cases and the like.

Clogs. Swedish wooden shoes, called *träskor*, have become a fashion hit around the world in recent years. They are available here in a wide assortment of models.

Cameras. A good buy in Sweden, they include Hasselblad, the Swedish camera used in space by the American astronauts.

Sporting Goods. Outdoor lovers will enjoy browsing in Stockholm's many sports shops. Among the interesting items: first-rate camping equipment and rods and reels made by ABU, the Swedish company that has become one of the world's biggest exporters of high-quality fishing gear.

Candles. To create a cozy mood during the long winter nights, the Swedes use a staggering number of candles in their homes. You'll find them in all imaginable sizes, shapes and colours, and, of course, the **83**

Swedish glassware, known the world over, is one of the best buys in town.

variety of candlesticks—in all kinds of materials from glass and metal to wood and straw—is equally broad.

Christmas Decorations. In Sweden Christmas is still celebrated with a great deal of tradition, and the yuletide ornaments make very attractive souvenirs. Most of the larger department stores have rea-lized this fact and offer tourists a small selection of these holiday items all year long.

Food. Just before leaving, why not buy some Swedish cheese, herring, caviar, smoked salmon, crisp bread and—last but not least—a bottle of aqua-vit, so that you can treat your friends back home to a little *smörgåsbord.*

Sports

The Swedes are a very sports-minded people, so it's not surprising that good sporting facilities are found throughout the Stockholm region. Top spectator sports are soccer in the summer, and ice hockey in the winter. Prestigious sporting events, such as ice hockey championships, are held in the Globe Arena, whose gigantic white dome you must have noticed on the city's south horizon. Said to be the largest spherical building in the world, the Arena can be converted rapidly from sports stadium to theatre or concert hall.

All kinds of water sports—sailing, swimming and fishing—are popular, as you would expect in a city that virtually floats on water. Swedes of all ages are also fond of jogging and cross-country skiing, and there are many such trails in the wooded areas around the city. Stop at the Stockholm Information Service (see p. 124) for up-to-date information.

Swimming. The Stockholm region boasts 125 miles of beaches—both sea and lake bathing—including several at Riddarfjärden near the centre of town. But keep in mind that the water seldom gets very warm (above 68°F). If this is too cold for you there are seven outdoor pools in the city, some with saunas, and dozens of others in the suburbs, open from May to mid-September. One of the oldest and nicest pools, Vanadisbadet, near Sveavägen, has been converted into a beautiful water park with slides; the biggest is Eriksdalsbadet, on the south side of the city, which can accommodate 3,000 persons. Note: nude bathing is not allowed at the pools.

Fishing. Pollution has been eliminated from Stockholm waters in the last few years, and it's now possible to catch salmon in Strömmen, the stream that flows past the Royal Palace. There is good fishing in Lake Mälaren, the smaller lakes in the city environs and around the 24,000 islands of the archipelago in the Baltic Sea. Fishing permits are required but easy to obtain. Check with the Stockholm Information Service.

Sailing. Sailing enthusiasts will find lots of company in Stockholm. In the summer, there are almost as many boats as cars—in Lake Mälaren, in the Baltic, and skimming through the city waterways. There are at least 10 different places in the Stockholm area where boats can be rented **85**

Do as the Swedes do; profit from the great outdoor possibilities.

(again, check with the tourist office), and also special harbours for visitors who come with their own boats. A note of caution: if you plan to sail through the labyrinth of islands that make up the Stockholm archipelago, you had better know what you're doing. It's a beautiful sailing experience, but not for amateurs.

Golf. This is a growing sport in Sweden. There are about 200 courses in the country, including one beyond the Arctic Circle where it's possible to play under the light of the midnight sun. In the Stockholm area the following 27-hole golf courses stand out: Djursholms Golfklubb, Saltsjöbadens Golfklubb, Ågesta Golfklubb and Lindö Golfklubb. And of the 18-hole courses: Ullna Golfklubb (Åkersberga), Lidingö Golfklubb, Stockholms Golf-

klubb (Kevinge) and Wärmdö Golf & Country Club. Be sure to phone the club first, especially on weekends, to check on teeing-off times.

Tennis. The fantastic success of native son Björn Borg did a lot to popularize tennis in Sweden. You might have some trouble getting time on a court evenings and weekends, but otherwise it should be all right. Two very good places, with indoor and outdoor courts, are Kungliga Tennishallen, Liding-övägen 75, and Tennisstadion, Fiskartorpsvägen 20. **Squash** is also quite popular.

Hiking. The hallowed tradition of *allemansrätten* guarantees everyone an equal right to enjoy nature. That means that you can walk just about anywhere in Sweden, in the woods and meadows, gathering flowers and mushrooms and berries, as long as you don't damage anyone else's property. But for those in search of more organized itineraries, there are **87**

marked trails starting just outside of Stockholm. Ambitious hikers can follow a trail called "Upplandsleden", from Järfälla to Uppsala and from Bålsta to Enköping. Another, east of Stockholm, "Roslagsleden", leads from Danderyd to Domarudden (56 km).

Horse-racing. There are two tracks—Täby, for flat racing and jumping, and Solvalla, a first-rate course for trotting, with a restaurant where you can place bets and watch the action while enjoying a meal.

Soccer. The big matches, invariably played before large, howling crowds, take place at the Råsunda and Stockholm stadiums.

Skating. The most popular, and conspicuous, outdoor rink is in Kungsträdgården in the very centre of town. But many Swedes prefer long-distance skating along the frozen waterways of Lake Mälaren and the Baltic Sea.

Many other recreational possibilities are centred in Djurgården, where you can hire a bike, go horseback riding and enjoy a number of peaceful promenades.

Riders enjoy trails of Djurgården; Drottningholm Theatre stages 18th-century operas and ballets.

Entertainment

No one would claim that the entertainment possibilities in Stockholm are equal to those of, say, New York or London. But there's enough going on in this town to satisfy the desires of visitors. And the long, light Stockholm summer nights are made to order for all kinds of pleasurable outdoor activities. *Stockholm This Week*, published by the Stockholm Information Service, is an in-dispensable guide to what's happening in the city. It's available free at your hotel.

Music and Theatre

Headquarters for serious music during the winter months is the big auditorium of the Stockholm Konserthuset. In the summer you can enjoy **concerts** in many splendid settings throughout the Stockholm area—in the Royal Palace, in the courtyard of the Hallwylska Museet, at Prince

Eugen's Waldemarsudde, in St. Jacob's Church and the German Church in the Old Town. There are also open-air concerts in many of the city parks, including Kungsträdgården in the heart of town.

A very long season (early fall to late spring) of absolutely first-rate **opera** and **ballet** is offered at Operan (the Royal Opera). In the summer the scene shifts to the unique Drottningholm Court Theatre (see pp. 69–70) for productions of 17th- and 18th-century opera and ballet. Also check to see if the Cullberg Ballet Company, an excellent troupe of dancers formed by choreographer Birgit Cullberg, is performing during your stay in Stockholm.

Modern and classical **plays** are staged at Kungliga Dramatiska Teatern and Stadsteatern (the Stockholm Municipal Theatre)—in Swedish only. The Marionette Theatre offers outstanding puppet and marionette productions for children and adults.

There are many **cinemas** in the centre, and all foreign films are shown in their original language with Swedish subtitles. But if you want to see a Bergman film where it was made, you'll have to struggle along with the Swedish.

Top spots for **jazz** are the Stampen, a pub in the Old Town and Fasching Jazzclub at Kungsgatan. Stockholm Jazz and Blues Festival is held the last weekend in June and first weekend in July on Skeppsholmen.

Nightlife

Night people will be pleased to know that the sidewalks in Stockholm are no longer rolled up at midnight. Many **nightclubs,** including a few at hotels, now stay open until 3 a.m. All have live dance music; some, cabaret and variety shows. If you sit at a table you are expected to eat, but at the bar ordering food is unnecessary. There are also about 50 **dance restaurants** in town that close earlier, around 1 a.m. Note: since unattached males and unescorted females are the rule rather than the exception at Stockholm dance restaurants and nightclubs, these are good places to meet people.

They come and go, and sometimes change names, but **discos** are always around. In Stockholm they usually charge an entrance fee—quite high—and cater mainly for the blue jeans set.

The Swedes have long since become bored with **sex clubs**

(and porno cinemas), which now mainly attract foreign tourists. If you want to have a look, check *This Week in Stockholm* to see what's going on.

Parks

The famous open-air museum of **Skansen** (see pp. 48–50) mounts a full-summer season of all kinds of worthwhile outdoor entertainment. One evening it will be a performance by the Stockholm Philharmonic Orchestra, the next a group of Swedish fiddlers or a foreign dance troupe. You can also dine and dance in Skansen's first-class restaurant.

Skansen's neighbour, **Gröna Lund,** is another focal point of good summer entertainment. Crowds flock to the amusement park's open-air stage to see performances by interna-

Big wheel: traditional fairgrounds highlight whirls above Gröna Lund.

tional artists, which have included such diverse figures as Birgit Nilsson, Count Basie and Sven-Bertil Taube, Sweden's popular modern troubadour.

Festivals

The Swedes may be ultra-modern in their social and sexual attitudes, but they are very traditional when it comes to holiday celebrations. Throughout the year in all parts of the country, festivals of various kinds brighten up the calendar.

One of the winter highlights is **St. Lucia Day,** a beguiling pre-Christmas ceremony observed on December 13. Young girls dressed in long white gowns are crowned with wreaths of lighted candles that symbolize light breaking into the winter darkness. They sing a special Lucia song and serve fresh buns and coffee. If you're in Sweden on this day, you'll see lighted candles on the tables of practically every coffee shop and restaurant.

As in most countries, Christmas and Easter are religious holidays in Lutheran Sweden, but **Walpurgis Night,** on April 30, has its roots in the paganism of Viking times. Huge bonfires blaze across the landscape to salute the arrival of spring. The celebration is especially exuberant in university towns, where the students hold torchlight parades and toast spring in verse, speeches and song.

May Day is given over to labour groups, and on **June 6** the Swedish National Day is celebrated with flags, parades and supersonic jets streaking across the sky.

On the longest day of the year—**Midsummer Eve,** the Friday between June 19 and 25—colourful maypoles decorated with garlands of birch boughs and wildflowers are raised in most village and town squares all over Sweden. After the maypole goes up, everyone joins hands and dances around it to the tunes of country fiddlers. The dancing, and a fair amount of drinking and merry-making, usually continues far into the night, which in midsummer is as bright as day. Also, as legend has it, if a girl picks seven different kinds of wildflowers and places them under her pillow she'll dream of her future husband.

In Stockholm, Midsummer Eve festivities are held at Skansen, and you're welcome to join in on the fun.

At Skansen traditionally costumed dancers join hands around the maypole in Midsummer Eve celebration.

Dining and Drinks

Natural is the best way to describe the Swedish approach to food. A Swede can become lyrical at the thought of *färskpotatis*, new potatoes boiled with dill (a much-used herb here) and served simply with a pat of butter. Wild berries and mushrooms are also highly prized, especially since food prices have skyrocketed in recent years.

Swedish law gives every man the right to wander through field and forest to pick these gifts of nature for himself. So even city dwellers, who are never too far away from the great outdoors, take full advantage of this opportunity to gather *smultron* (wild strawberries), *blåbär* (bilberries, or blueberries), *lingon* (wild cranberries), *hjortron* (Arctic cloudberries) and *svamp* (mushrooms).

In Sweden each season has its traditional specialities, and any discussion of eating habits has to take these into account.* Some regional dishes, like blood soup and fermented herring, may sound a bit unappetizing, but tourists with an adventurous palate will want to try at least a few of those things which the calendar and time-honoured custom prescribe.

Spring and Summer Specialities

As the name implies, *fettisdagsbullar* or *semlor* (Shrove Tuesday buns) are associated with Lent, but they have become so popular nowadays that they appear on the market right after Christmas. A rather strange concoction, the baked buns are split, filled with almond paste and whipped cream and then served in a deep dish with hot milk, sugar and cinnamon. The arrival of spring is traditionally celebrated with another calorie-packed treat, *våfflor* (crisp waffles served with jam and whipped cream), as well as three salmon delicacies—*gravad lax*, pickled salmon in dill served with mustard sauce, *färskrökt lax*, smoked salmon, and *kokt lax*, boiled salmon.

Summertime means almost 24-hour daylight in Sweden. And it's a season when people in this northern clime can luxuriate in fruit and vegetables that have been grown locally under the midnight sun, instead of the expensive imported produce available during much of the year. Look for *västkustsallad*, a delicious sea-

---

* For a comprehensive guide to dining in Sweden, consult the Berlitz EUROPEAN MENU READER.

food salad with mushrooms and tomatoes.

A delightful custom not to be missed by anyone visiting Sweden in August is the *kräftor* (crayfish) party. Donning paper bibs, the usually proper Swede abandons all rules of table etiquette as he attacks the piles of small lobster-like creatures gleaming bright red in the light of the gay paper lanterns strung over the table. *Kryddost*, cheese spiced with caraway, and buttered toast

A classic smörgåsbord can consist of as many as 100 different dishes.

and fresh berries complete the traditional menu. The mood can become quite festive, especially since liberal amounts of aquavit are usually downed on this occasion.

This highly potent drink accompanies another seasonal speciality, *surströmming* (salted and fermented Baltic herring). Many people, in fact, can't get this fish past their nose without the aid of a dram or two of aquavit. The smell, to put it mildly, is staggering, but there are Swedes, particularly those from the northern part of the country, who consider it a great delicacy.

Fall and Winter Fare

Though southern Sweden is the best place to celebrate St. Martin's Day, you can usually find a few restaurants in Stockholm that observe the tradition as well. The star of this November event is *stekt gås* (roast goose), but the first course and dessert probably deserve the most attention. You begin the meal with a highly spiced *svartsoppa* (blood soup) and finish with *spettekaka*, a lace-like pyramid cake baked on a spit. It literally melts in your mouth.

The Christmas season gets off to an early, and charming, start in Sweden on December 13—one of the darkest and shortest days of the year—when Lucia makes her early morning appearance in many homes and even public places. Dressed in a long, white robe and with a crown of lighted candles on her head, the Queen of Light awakens the sleeping house by singing the special Lucia song and serving saffron buns, ginger snaps and coffee.

Christmas is preceded by weeks of preparation in the kitchen. Even now, when so many Swedish housewives hold down full-time jobs outside the home, the old customs survive. The Yuletide *smörgåsbord (julbord)* in private homes may be somewhat pared down these days, but none of the essential ingredients are left out. And restaurants often make a special feature of the *smörgåsbord* at Christmas time.

But the *smörgåsbord* is only part of the Swedish holiday menu. Other dishes are *lutfisk* (cod that has been dried and cured in lye), *risgrynsgröt* (rice porridge containing one almond destined for the person to be wed in the coming year) and *skinka* (ham). This time of year also brings forth all kinds of delicious breads and pastries.

97

The Smörgåsbord

Bounded by the sea and with some 96,000 lakes dotting the countryside, Sweden has an abundant supply of fish, which quite naturally plays an important role in the country's diet. In the old days fish was often dried, smoked, cured or fermented to preserve it for the winter. But even today, in the age of the deep-freeze, these methods are among the favourite ways of preparing herring and other treasures from the sea. And the herring buffet, or *sillbord,* the predecessor of the *smörgåsbord,* still forms the backbone of Sweden's most famous culinary attraction.

The *smörgåsbord* table (or groaning board, if you will), can consist of as many as 100 different dishes. It should not be tackled haphazardly. The first thing to remember is not to overload your plate—you can go back to the table as many times as you wish.

Even more important is the order in which you eat. Start off by sampling the innumerable herring dishes, taken with boiled potatoes and bread and butter. Then you move on to other seafood, like smoked or boiled salmon, smoked eel, Swedish caviar, shrimps, etc. Next come the delightful egg dishes, cold meats (try the smoked reindeer) and salads. The small warm dishes now loom on the horizon—such as meat balls, fried sausages and omelets—and finally (if you still have room) you end up with cheese and fruit.

Breakfast and Bread

Breakfast *(frukost)* usually consists of a cup of coffee or tea with rolls, butter and marmalade and sometimes cheese. But a more substantial breakfast, with eggs, bacon or ham, will certainly be available at your hotel.

Coffee—excellent in Sweden—is consumed in great quantities at all times of the day and night and forms a recognized part of Swedish social life. The Swedes, even adults, drink a lot of milk with their meals. They also like yoghurt and other kinds of fermented milk.

Until quite recently many people complained that Swedish bread (which contains molasses) was too sweet. But unsweetened bread is now widely sold. Be sure to try *knäckebröd* (crisp rye bread), which comes in a wide assortment. This might be something to take back home, along with some cheese—there are, reportedly, more than 200 different kinds to choose from in Swe-

den. Look for *västerbotten-ost*, *herrgårdsost* and *svecia-ost*—typical hard, well-aged cheeses.

Restaurants

During recent years pizzerias, hamburger chains and Chinese restaurants have spread like wildfire in the Stockholm area. And there are many others specializing in the food of France, Germany, Spain, Hungary, Greece and so on. The real problem nowadays is finding

Dining al fresco in Djurgården can be a delightful experience.

genuine, old-fashioned Swedish food.

Keep your eye open for restaurants that make a point of serving *husmanskost*—traditional everyday Swedish dishes. Among these you might try: *Janssons frestelse* (Jansson's Temptation), a delicious casserole of potatoes, sprats, onion and cream; *kåldolmar*, **99** stuffed cabbage rolls; *pytt i panna,* finely cut meat, onions and potatoes; *kalops,* beef stew; *dillkött,* lamb or veal in dill sauce; *köttbullar,* the famous Swedish meatballs; *bruna bönor,* baked brown beans in molasses sauce; *strömmingsflundror,* fried boned herring; and on Thursday, join almost the entire local populace in eating *ärter med fläsk,* yellow pea soup with pork, followed by *pannkakor med sylt,* pancakes with jam.

The *smörgåsbord* is also hard to find, except on Sunday afternoons and during the Christmas season. In Stockholm the elegant Operakällaren (the Opera Restaurant) offers a daily luncheon *smörgåsbord,* reputed to be the best in the world. Otherwise, ask the receptionist at your hotel for advice on this subject.

Eating out in Stockholm is not exactly cheap, but prices at the top-flight restaurants are generally in line with comparable establishments in other European cities. Having pre-dinner cocktails in a restaurant or bar, on the other hand, can make a real dent in your budget. The best thing is to have wine or beer with your meal.

There are many inexpensive self-service cafeterias scattered throughout the city, and most restaurants have small portions for children at half price. Also look for the *Dagens rätt* (Today's Special), usually a good bet.

Lunch is served around noon, and dinner from 6 p.m. A 13 per cent service charge is normally added to the restaurant bill, but the waiter or waitress will expect (or hope for) a small extra tip.

Alcoholic Beverages

The Swedish national drink is aquavit, also called *snaps,* distilled from potatoes or grain and flavoured with various herbs and spices. There are many varieties. Aquavit should always be consumed with food, especially herring; it should be ice-cold and served in small glasses, taken straight in a grand gulp or two and washed down with beer or mineral water. Aquavit is closely linked to the word *skål,* that universally recognized Scandinavian toast uttered while looking straight into the eyes of your drinking companion.

Other Swedish alcoholic specialities include *glögg,* a hot, spiced wine that appears during the Christmas season, and *punsch* (punch), usually served after dinner, well chilled, with coffee. It can also be drunk hot with the traditional Thursday dinner of yellow pea soup and pancakes.

Teetotaller organizations are a powerful factor in Swedish politics, and this has led to very high taxes on alcoholic beverages, especially hard liquor, as a means of discouraging drinking. Also, with the exception of a very weak beer that can be bought in grocery stores or supermarkets, alcoholic beverages are sold only in the shops of the Systembolaget, the state-owned liquor monopoly.

These shops have everything in the way of well-known brands of whisky, vodka, gin, etc., but wine is by far the best buy. Popular table wines (French, Italian, Spanish and Greek) are shipped to Sweden in huge tankers and bottled here. The quality is good, the selection wide and the prices are relatively moderate. It all ties in with the Systembolaget campaign to promote the drinking of wine (in moderate quantities, of course) while at the same time propagandizing about the evils of consuming hard liquor.

To Help You Order...

Could we have a table?
Do you have a set menu?

Finns det något ledigt bord?
Har ni någon meny?

I'd like a/an/some...

Jag skulle vilja ha...

beer	**öl**	meat	**kött**
(weak)	**lättöl**	menu	**matsedeln**
(strong)	**starköl**	milk	**mjölk**
bread	**bröd**	mineral water	**mineralvatten**
butter	**smör**	mustard	**senap**
cheese	**ost**	pepper	**peppar**
coffee	**kaffe**	potatoes	**potatis**
cream	**grädde**	salad	**sallad**
dessert	**efterrätt**	salt	**salt**
egg	**ägg**	sandwich	**smörgås**
fish	**fisk**	soup	**soppa**
fruit	**frukt**	sugar	**socker**
glass	**glas**	tea	**te**
ice-cream	**glass**	wine	**vin**

ansjovis	marinated sprats	njure	kidney
bakad potatis	baked potatoes	nyponsoppa	rose hip soup
biff	beefsteak	oxrulader	braised rolls of sliced beef
böckling	smoked herring		
fiskbullar	fish balls	oxstek	roast beef
fläskkotlett	pork chop	paj	pie
fläskpann- kaka	(oven-baked) pan- cake with pork	pannbiff	minced beef
		pepparrots- kött	boiled beef with horseradish sauce
fromage	mousse		
fruktsallad	fruit salad		
gryta	casserole, stew	potatismos	mashed potatoes
gädda	pike	rabarber	rhubarb
gös	pike-perch	rensadel	saddle of rein- deer
hallon	raspberries		
höns	stewing chicken	revbensspjäll	spare ribs
isterband	smoked sausage	rotmos	mashed turnips
jordgubbar	strawberries	rulltårta	Swiss (jelly) roll
järpe	grouse or ground meat dumpling	råbiff	beef tartare
		rådjurssadel	saddle of veni- son
kalv	veal	räkor	shrimps
kasseler	smoked pork loin	rödbetor	beet(root)
		röding	char (fish)
kokt	boiled	rödspätta	plaice
korv	sausage	sillbullar	herring rissoles
krabba	crab	sjömansbiff	beef and potato stew made with beer
krusbär	gooseberries		
kyckling	chicken		
köttfärssås	minced meat sauce		
		skaldjur	shellfish
		skinka	ham
lammstek	roast lamb	sparris	asparagus
lax	salmon	spenat	spinach
laxpudding	potatoes and sal- mon gratin	stekt	fried
		stuvad	creamed
lever	liver	tonfisk	tuna fish
löjrom	vendace roe	tårta	layer cake
lök	onion	vitkål	(white) cabbage
makrill	mackerel	ål	eel
matjessill	pickled herring	älg	elk
musslor	mussels, clams	äppelkaka	apple cake

102

BLUEPRINT for a Perfect Trip

How to Get There

Because of the complexity and variability of the many fares, you should ask the advice of an informed travel agent well before your departure.

BY AIR

Scheduled flights

Stockholm's Arlanda Airport (see p.108), the main gateway to Sweden, is linked by regular flights from numerous European and several North American cities. Connecting service from cities throughout Europe and from North America and the Middle and Far East operates via Copenhagen Airport. The flight from London to Stockholm takes approximately 2½ hours, from New York to Stockholm, 10½ hours.

Charter flights and package tours

From the U.K. and Ireland: Charter flights and package tours to Sweden are highly uncommon, but within Sweden there are various attractive packages. Ask for up-to-date information at a reliable travel agency when you reach Sweden—the types of tickets are constantly changing.

From North America: Stockholm is featured on GITs (Group Inclusive Tours) of 15 days or longer. Some tours offer 2 days of visits in the city before a boat trip through the Norwegian Fjords. Several packages are available to Scandinavia plus Lapland and the North Cape. GIT includes round-trip air transport, hotel accommodation, meals as specified, transfers, baggage handling, ground transport, the services of an English-speaking guide, plus service charges and taxes.

For visitors from North America and the Far East there's also the advantageous Visit Scandinavia plan; inquire at a travel agency before leaving home.

BY SEA AND ROAD

Many people find the ferry services to Sweden inexpensive and comfortable. You can travel with or without your car from Harwich or Newcastle to Gothenburg. The journey lasts about 24 hours, but book in advance, especially for summer crossings. Remember that your car must be on the quay 1 hour before sailing time. The E20 (formerly E3) is the most direct route from Gothenburg to Stockholm, but you can also follow smaller scenic roads on the way. Various package holidays, generally designed for motorists, include the boat trip plus all sorts of accommodation from camping and cabins to hotels. Those travelling without a car can make connections from Gothenburg by train. Other inexpensive means of travel are express buses, postal cars and Swedish Railways' inter-city weekend bus service.

The main access route from continental Europe is by car ferry from Puttgarden on the north German island of Fehmarn to Rødbyhavn on the Danish island of Lolland. Then continue on via Copenhagen to Elsinore (Helsingør) for another ferry crossing to Helsingborg in Sweden and take the E4 to Stockholm. Another possibility is to take the 12-hour car-ferry from Kiel in northern Germany to Gothenburg in Sweden and drive the 520 km. (320 mi.) to Stockholm. Other ferry crossings between north Germany and Sweden are Travemünde–Trelleborg or Malmö.

BY RAIL

You can travel from London to Stockholm by train via Harvich–the Hook (Holland) or Dover–Ostend, then on to Sweden by way of Copenhagen (Hook–Stockholm takes 22-25 hours, Ostend–Gothenburg–Stockholm 26-28 hours).

The main rail route from Central Europe is the Lübeck–Puttgarden–Rødbyhavn–Copenhagen stretch (see above).

The **Inter-Rail Card** is valid for one month's unlimited second-class travel in Europe for youths under 26. The **Rail Europ S** (senior) card, obtainable before departure only, entitles senior citizens to purchase train tickets for European destinations at reduced prices.

People living outside Europe and North Africa can purchase a **Eurailpass** for unlimited travel in 16 European countries including Sweden. This pass must be obtained before leaving home.

Within Sweden, visitors can purchase various rail bargains: **SJ Sverige-kort** (Sweden Card) permits 1st- and 2nd-class travel during one year at a discount that varies according to the day of travel. Finally, the **Nordic Tourist Ticket** allows unlimited travel on Swedish and orther Scandinavian trains for 21 days (and 50% discount on boats to Finland and the island of Åland). There are also some rail tours with unlimited stopovers, including Stockholm.

When to Go

Summer is, of course, prime season to visit Stockholm. In midsummer, daylight lasts up to 19 hours with lots of sunshine—and lots of other visitors. In the spring, particularly lovely in the lake district and outlying regions, and autumn, with bright colours and clear nights, you'll have Sweden to yourself. Winter is tempting for sports enthusiasts and Christmas in Sweden can be an unforgettable experience.

The following charts will give you an idea of the average daily maximum and minimum temperatures and average number of rainy days each month in Stockholm.

		J	F	M	A	M	J	J	A	S	O	N	D
Max.	°F	31	31	37	45	57	65	70	66	58	48	38	33
	°C	−1	−1	3	7	14	18	21	19	14	9	3	1
Min.	°F	23	22	26	32	41	49	55	53	46	39	31	26
	°C	−5	−6	−3	0	5	9	13	12	8	4	−1	−3
Days of rainfall		10	7	6	7	7	8	9	10	9	9	10	11

Planning Your Budget

The following are some prices in Swedish kronor (kr). However, they must be regarded as approximate as inflation is running high.

Airport transfer. Airport bus to city centre 50 kr, SAS limousine service 800 kr per car. Taxi 200 kr.

Boat trips (return fares). Stockholm to Gripsholm 160 kr, to Sandhamn 90 kr, to Birka 105 kr, to Drottningholm 55 kr.

Camping. 65–75 kr per person.

Car hire. *Ford Sierra* (automatic) 390 kr per day, 100 km. free, then 13 kr per 10 km. *Saab 9000 Turbo* 610 kr per day, 2.75 kr per km. *Saab 9000* 885 kr for 24 hours, unlimited mileage.

Entertainment. Concerts 75–300 kr, opera 75–300 kr, theatre 75–300 kr, cinema 60 kr, nightclub/discotheque entry 60 kr.

Guided tours. Boat cruise under Stockholm's bridges (1 hour), adults 50 kr, children 6–12 years ½ price. City sightseeing tour (2½ hours with bus) adults 150 kr, children 75 kr.

Guides. 654 kr for first three hours, 218 kr for each additional hour, plus booking fee 150 kr.

Hairdressers. *Man's* haircut 150–200 kr. *Woman's* cut 200–250 kr, shampoo and set 250 kr, blow-dry 150 kr, rinse/dye 200–250 kr.

Hotels (double room with bath per night). Luxury 1,900–2,400 kr and up, 1st class 800–900 kr, budget 450–600 kr. Prices include breakfast, service and tax *(moms)*. Youth hostels 111 kr and up, sheets 40 kr per person.

Meals and drinks. Continental breakfast 45 kr, lunch 55–65 kr, dinner in fairly good establishment 150–200 kr, coffee 15 kr, light beer 20 kr, export beer 40–50 kr, cocktail 70 kr, bottle of wine 100 kr and up, 4 cl. *snaps* 40 kr, 4 cl. whisky 40 kr.

Museums. 20–25 kr.

Public transport. Single ticket 10 kr; card of 15 units 55 kr, 1-day tourist card: zone one 28 kr, Stockholm Country 50 kr; 3-day tourist card 95 kr (including Skansen, Kaknästornet, Gröna Lund and for all cards the Djugård Ferry and Tramway Museum, but not the tram).

Stockholm Card. 24 hours 135 kr, 2×24 hours 270 kr, 3×24 hours 405 kr (2 children 7–17 years included).

Taxis. Basic charge 40 kr, plus 15 kr per km.

Trains (2nd class). Stockholm–Uppsala 60 kr one way, 120 kr return.

An A–Z Summary of Practical Information and Facts

> Listed after may entries is an equivalent Swedish translation, usually in the singular. A star (*) after an entry title indicates that prices concerning this section can be found on page 107.

A

AIRPORTS* *(flygplats).* All flights to Stockholm are handled by Arlanda Airport, 38 kilometres from the city. The airport telephone number is 08-797 00 00.

Arlanda's international terminal has a first-class restaurant, self-service buffet, bar, Swedish food shop, gift boutiques, duty-free shop, news- and book-stands as well as a post office, bank and nursery. There are also car-hire desks and tourist information booths where you can book accommodation.

Although taxis are plentiful they are expensive, and for one-eighth the fare you can take an airport bus into town (which takes about 40 minutes). These buses make three stops: near a motor hotel at Ulriksdals trafikplats, on the northern outskirts of the city; St Eriksplan; and Cityterminalen, near the railway station in the city centre.

Note: Since the Cityterminalen stop was introduced the taxi service has improved considerably, and you no longer need to get off at Haga, where the taxis used to be more plentiful.

Domestic flights. Domestic routes are served by Linjeflyg and SAS and operate from the Arlanda domestic terminal, linked to the international terminal by a 300-metre walkway.

B

BOATS*. Stockholm and its environs are made to order for boat excursions. Sightseeing boats cruise under the city's bridges, steamers serve the islands of the archipelago in the Baltic and ply the waters of Lake Mälaren, making stops at Drottningholm Palace, Gripsholm Castle and other noteworthy places. Tours range from a one-hour trip in the city to a long cruise with a stay overnight in Sandhamn on the island of Sandön. Private companies offer a wide choice of excursions which are listed at the Stockholm Information Service.

Yachting. If you're a seasoned sailor and would like to rent a boat you should know the regulations which apply to Swedish territorial waters and where guest harbours are located. Get in touch with the Swedish Touring Club (STF):

Box 25, Drottninggatan 31–33, 101 20 Stockholm, tel. 08-790 31 00.

Canoeing is a popular sport in Sweden and even in Stockholm you can hire a canoe. Contact:

Svenska Kanotförbundet, Skeppsbron 11, 611 35 Nyköping.
Tel. 0155-69508.

CAMPING *. Sweden has more than 500 camping sites that are officially approved and rated by one, two and three stars, according to facilities offered. In the vicinity of Stockholm are Bredäng Camping (about 15 minutes' drive north of the centre of town), Rösjön in Sollentuna and Ängby Camping in the suburb of Bromma. For a complete list of sites get a copy of "Campingboken" (The Camping Book) published by the Swedish Tourist Board, available at any Swedish bookshop.

If you don't have an International Camping Card you can get a Swedish card issued by Sveriges Campingvärdars Riksförbund (SCR) for only a few kronor at campsites in Sweden, along with a free camping guide. Camping cheques are valid in most sites and allow you to stay at reduced rates. Upon purchase, you get complete information on different sites and surrounding areas. Before leaving home get in touch with the Swedish Tourist Board's representative.

Cabins for rent (with beds) are very reasonable, too. You use your own sleeping bag but kitchen facilities are usually provided. Ask for a list at any campsite in Sweden.

According to the tradition of *allemansrätten* (Everyman's Right), visitors may camp for one night on any private property without the owner's permission (not with caravan), but there are exceptions, so it's always best to ask. Make sure that tents are not pitched too close to dwellings or gardens and that the grounds are left undamaged and unlittered.

CHILDREN'S ACTIVITIES. Kids can have a lot of fun in Stockholm. Gröna Lund, the amusement park, has rides; the zoo at Skansen has a special section with baby farm animals children can pet. Many museums have special sections for children. At Kulturhuset youngsters of any age can make clogs, pottery or other handicrafts.

The royal ship *Wasa* has been restored and offers a unique occasion to observe what life at sea was like in the 17th century.

Finally, the archipelago with its countless islets can be reached by regular boat services from Stockholm, and many children ask for nothing better than to climb among the rocks, fish or swim.

CIGARETTES, CIGARS, TOBACCO *(cigarett, cigarr, tobak)*. Smoking is an expensive habit in Sweden, but virtually all international brands of cigarettes are available in tobacco shops and kiosks. Local cigarette brands are quite good, and Sweden is especially known for its quality pipe tobaccos. You can also buy cigarettes and cigars in the bigger restaurants, where a small extra charge is usually added.

Smoking is prohibited on all public transport (apart from a few reserved areas) and in many other public places as well.

CLOTHING. The weather in Stockholm is often ideal in the summer, pleasantly warm with low humidity. Evenings can be a bit cool, requiring a sweater or shawl.

In spring and fall a light overcoat or raincoat will come in handy, and of course winter requires warm boots and coats, according to your planned activities.

Stockholmers no longer dress up like they used to, and even at the theatre, concert or opera casual clothes are the rule. A few late-opening restaurants require (or expect) guests to wear a tie and jacket.

It's clear you should bring appropriate shoes for walking if you're planning to visit the Old Town and city parks. Hiking clothes include sturdy boots, a warm sweater, and waterproof clothing.

The following chart should help you to choose sizes if you plan to purchase clothing in Sweden:

Men						
Clothing		Shirts		Shoes		
GB/USA	Swed.	GB/USA	Swed.	GB	USA	Swed.
34	44	14	36	7	7½	40
36	46	15	38	7½	8	41
38	48	16	40	8	8½	42
40	50	17	42	9	9½	43
42	52	17½	43	10	10½	44

Women								
Clothing			Shirts/Pullovers			Shoes		
GB	USA	Swed.	GB	USA	Swed.	GB	USA	Swed.
10	8	36	32	10	38			
12	10	38	34	12	40	4	5½	36
14	12	40	36	14	42	5	6½	37
16	14	42	38	16	44	6	7½	38
18	16	44	40	18	46	6½	8	38½
20	18	46	42	20	48	7	8½	39

COMMUNICATIONS. Unlike certain other European countries the post office only handles mail; for telephone and telegram or telex services you have to go to the "Tele" offices.

Post Office *(postkontor)*. The main office is not far from the Central Railway Station at Vasagatan 28–34. To receive your mail poste restante (general delivery) have it sent to the Central Post Office, Stockholm 1. Stamps and aerogrammes can be bought either at the post office or at tobacco shops, kiosks, department stores and hotels.

You'll find a yellow sign with a blue horn outside every post office. Letterboxes are also yellow.

Telephone *(telefon)*, **Telegrams and Telex.** All phones have fully automatic dial systems and are conveniently located in glass-enclosed sidewalk stalls and in "Tele" offices (see below). Dialling instructions are in Swedish and English. You can dial directly to most cities in Europe and the U.S.A. To call Britain from Sweden dial the prefix 00944; for the U.S. it's 0091 from Stockholm. Reduced rates apply to the U.S. and Canada from 10 p.m. to 10 a.m. and all day Sunday. For overseas information call 0019.

Public phone and telegraph offices (marked "Tele") offer telex as well as telegram and telephone services. The main office in Stockholm, open daily from early morning until midnight, is located at Skeppsbron 2. You can also send a telegram by phoning 0021.

airmail	**flygpost**
special delivery	**express**
poste restante	**poste restante**
registered	**rekommenderat**

C **CONVERTER CHARTS.** For fluid and distance measures, see page 114. Sweden uses the metric system.

Temperature

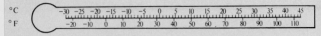

Length

Weight

grams	0	100	200	300	400	500	600	700	800	900	1 kg
ounces	0		4	8	12	1 lb	20	24	28	2 lb.	

CRIME and THEFT. Stockholm, like other cities, has kept up with the times, which means that crime has increased. You're not likely to get mugged or have your purse snatched, but certain parts of the city, such as parks like Humlegården, can be a bit dangerous—or very unpleasant—late at night. It's a good idea to check your valuables in the hotel safe. Don't leave cameras and packages in view in your car, even if it's locked.

See also POLICE.

CUSTOMS and ENTRY FORMALITIES. Citizens of the U.S. and Canada need only a valid passport to enter Sweden, and British subjects can use their national identity card or British Visitor's Passport. There's no restriction on the amount of foreign or local currency you can bring into or take out of the country (provided it is declared upon entry).

The following chart indicates which other items you can take into **112** Sweden, and, when returning home, into your own country:

Into:	Cigarettes		Cigars		Tobacco	Spirits		Wine
Sweden 1)	200	or	50	or	250 g.	1 l.	and	1 l.
2)	400	or	100	or	500 g.	1 l.	and	1 l.
Australia	200	or	250 g.	or	250 g.	1 l.	or	1 l.
Eire	200	or	50	or	250 g.	1 l.	and	2 l.
N. Zealand	200	or	50	or	250 g.	1.1 l.	and	4.5 l.
S. Africa	400	and	50	and	250 g.	1 l.	and	2 l.
U.K.	200	or	50	or	250 g.	1 l.	and	2 l.
U.S.A.	200	and	100	and	3)	1 l.	or	1 l.

1) Residents of European countries.
2) Residents of non-European countries.
3) No restriction for personal use only.

CYCLING. Heavy traffic can make bicycling in Stockholm difficult, except for a few places like Djurgården, the big island park. You can hire a bicycle at Skepp och Hoch, a rental shop near Djurgårdsbron (the bridge leading to Djurgården).

Outside the city, especially in island provinces like Öland and Gotland where cycling's ideal, local tourist offices offer package deals which include accommodation and itineraries planned for you. Get in touch with Svenska Turistföreningen (the Swedish Touring Club) which has around 30 such package itineraries of varying length:

STF, Box 25, Drottninggatan 31–33, 101 20 Stockholm, tel. 08-790 31 00.

DRIVING IN SWEDEN. To take a car into Sweden you will need:

● National or international driving licence
● Car registration papers
● National identity sticker
● Green card or other internationally valid third party insurance.

Roads and Regulations: Drive on the right, pass on the left. Traffic on main roads and very often main streets in town have the right-of-way. Traffic on roundabouts usually has priority, but in other situations traffic from the right has the right-of-way.

D

It is obligatory to use seat belts, and that includes back-seat passengers if the car is so equipped. All vehicles (including motorcycles) must have dipped headlights switched on at all times, even in broad daylight.

Most Swedish roads are very good, though only a small proportion are motorways (expressways). On smaller roads you'll better appreciate Sweden's unspoiled environment. International pictographs are widely used, although you may see some signs in Swedish:

biljettautomat	ticket machine
bussfil	bus lane
busshållplats	bus-stop
ej genomfart	no through traffic
privat parkering	private parking

Routine spot checks to inspect driving licences and the condition of vehicles are quite common in Sweden. Police also check to see if drivers have been drinking, which is a very serious offense in Sweden. You can be fined or even sent to jail if your alcohol level exceeds 0.2 per mille.

Speed limits: Maximum speed limits are indicated by signs on all roads. On principal motorways (expressways) passenger vehicles can usually drive up to 110 kilometres per hour or 70 kph for a car towing a trailer. On other main roads outside built-up areas the speed limits are 90 or 70, depending on road width and traffic density. In towns it is 50 kph.

Fuel and oil: There are many petrol stations, most self-service. A lot of stations also have automatic pumps where you can fill up round-the-clock. This is all you may find open in the evening. The pumps work with 10- and 100-kronor notes and are indicated by the signs *Nattöppet* and *Sedelautomat*.

Fluid measures

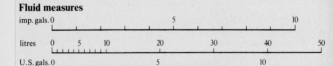

Distance

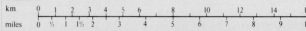

114

Parking: On main roads out of town parking is prohibited, but there are many places arranged for picnicking. In Stockholm parking meters indicate parking areas and there are also multi-level car parks.

Breakdowns: If you have serious car trouble you can either contact the police or call Larmtjänst (breakdown service), a company owned by the Swedish insurance companies. Their number in Stockholm is 08-241000. Otherwise, you can ring the following cheap-rate number from anywhere in Sweden: 020-910040. This connects you to the nearest office. Most of the bigger petrol stations also have mechanics on duty during the day.

Car Hire* *(biluthyrning):* All of the major international car hire agencies are represented in Stockholm, and there are reliable local firms as well. You can hire a car at Arlanda Airport when you arrive— or ask for a list at your hotel or travel bureau. Addresses are also in the business telephone directory called *Gula Sidorna* under "Biluthyrning".

To hire a car minimum age is 18. You'll need your driving licence and passport. Most companies require a deposit, but this is waived if you present an accepted credit card.

driving licence	**körkort**
car registration papers	**besiktningsinstrument**
Please check the oil/tires/battery.	**Kan ni kontrollera oljan/ däcken/batteriet, tack.**
I've had a breakdown.	**Bilen har gått sönder.**
There's been an accident.	**Det har hänt en olycka.**

ELECTRIC CURRENT. The voltage for electric appliances in Sweden is 220-volt, 50 cycles A.C.

EMBASSIES and CONSULATES *(ambassad; konsulat).* Following is a list of embassies and consulates in Stockholm:

Australia (Embassy): Sergels Torg 12, 103 86 Stockholm, tel. 613 29 60.

Canada (Embassy): Tegelbacken 4, 103 23 Stockholm, tel. 23 79 20.

Great Britain (Embassy with Consular section): Skarpögatan 6–8, 115 27 Stockholm, tel. 667 01 40.

United States (Embassy with Consular section): Strandvägen 101, 115 89 Stockholm, tel. 783 53 00.

E   **EMERGENCIES.** See also HEALTH AND MEDICAL CARE. The general emergency telephone number in Sweden is 90000. This number covers the police and fire departments, ambulance and medical services. It can be dialled free (no coins needed) from any telephone. English is usually understood.

If you fall ill or have an accident ask someone (e.g. hotel receptionist) to call a doctor for you, or go to a hospital's emergency and casualties reception *(akutmottagning)* or to City-Akuten, at Holländargatan 3, tel. 08-117177.

For emergency dental treatment go to the clinic called Akuttandvården at St. Eriks Sjukhus, Fleminggatan 22, 112 82 Stockholm, tel. 54 11 17 (8 a.m. to 7 p.m., telephone calls up to 9 p.m.).

Alternatively, you can ring Sjukvårdsupplysningen (44 92 00), a 24-hour service that will put you in touch with a dentist.

G   **GUIDES and INTERPRETERS*** *(guide; tolk).* The Swedish Tourist Board and the Stockholm Information Service can recommend excursions and trips. Sightseeing buses and boats have multilingual guides, and there are also guided tours in some museums. Authorized guides can be booked by ringing 789 24 31 any day of the week.

I'd like an English-speaking guide.   **Jag skulle vilja ha en guide som talar engelska.**

H   **HAIRDRESSERS*** *(frisör).* There are many beauty salons and barber shops in Stockholm, including those in the major hotels. Some offer service to both men and women. You should make an appointment by phone or drop by a salon and arrange for a time.

HEALTH and MEDICAL CARE. In the case of British subjects Sweden's national health insurance plan covers any illness or accidents which require doctors' services or hospitalization. This is due to a reciprocal agreement between the two countries. If you are not British you should check to see if your private insurance covers medical treatment in Sweden before leaving home.

Chemists' or drugstores are called *apotek;* they stock over-the-counter products like cough medicine or aspirin and fill prescriptions. A 24-hour pharmacy service is offered by C.W. Scheele at Klarabergsgatan 64 (near the Central Station), tel. 24 82 80.

Water *(vatten)* from the tap is perfectly safe to drink anywhere in Sweden. If you prefer mineral water, however, you'll find the local brands excellent and readily available. In remote mountain areas you can drink sparkling water straight from the lake or brook.

HOTELS and ACCOMMODATION* *(hotell; logi).*

Hotels in Stockholm, as elsewhere in Sweden, have a well-deserved reputation for cleanliness and good service, regardless of their price category. It may be difficult to find accommodation in Stockholm if you haven't booked in advance. Before leaving home, get a copy of the annual brochure published by the Swedish Tourist Board entitled "Hotels in Sweden" which has details about amenities and prices. Ask for it at the Swedish tourist office in your country or at your travel agency.

At the same time inquire about the Stockholm Package (including hotel, breakfast and the Stockholm Card) and the Hotel Cheque system, enabling you to get cut-rate prices at some 250 Swedish hotels. This last is especially useful if you plan to see some of the country outside of Stockholm. You can book your first night in Sweden before you leave home, then make reservations (free) for the following nights through the reception desk of each hotel. Children up to 12 stay free if they share the parents' bed. The Hotel Cheques are valid from mid-June to September 1. Note that many hotels offer special terms during the summer months and at weekends year round.

Should you arrive in Stockholm without having booked accommodation, get in touch with Hotellcentralen, run by the tourist office, to find a room in a hotel, boarding house or youth hostel. There's a bureau in the Arlanda Airport and at the Central Railway Station. They can be contacted by telephone at 24 08 80. During high season they're open every day until late at night; in low season during regular weekday hours.

Youth Hostels *(vandrarhem).*

Most of the youth hostels in Sweden are located in the southern and central parts of the country. They are cheap, comfortable and open to everyone irrespective of age. Most have hot and cold water in the rooms and showers, and many have special family rooms suitable for motorists with children under 16. You can bring your own sheets or buy them; sleeping bags are generally not allowed. One of the most unusual hostels is the *af Chapman,* a 19th-century sailing schooner permanently anchored at the Skeppsholmen quay in the centre of Stockholm.

If you're a member of an organization affiliated to the International Youth Hostel Federation, your card is valid in Sweden, and all Swed-

H ish hostels are listed in the IYHF handbook. For more information on Swedish hostels contact:

England: YHA Services, 14 Southampton Street, London WC2E 7HY.

Sweden: Svenska Turistföreningen (Swedish Touring Club), Drottninggatan 31–33, Stockholm, tel. 08-790 31 00.

U.S.A.: American Youth Hostels, Inc., National Campus, Delaplane, Virginia 22025.

The SSRS HOTELL DOMUS, a student organization, operates a *hotell-service* with rooms for rent during summer holidays at very reasonable rates. Their address:

Box 5906, Körsbärsvägen 1, 114 89 Stockholm, Sweden, tel. 08-16 01 95.

HOURS. Most shops and department stores are open from 9 or 9.30 a.m. to 6 p.m. on weekdays, until 1 p.m. on Saturdays (later in winter). Food shops have the same hours, but some supermarkets in major underground (subway) stations keep later hours and also open on Sunday afternoons. Certain food shops, *närbutiker,* can be open from either 7 a.m. to 11 p.m. or 10 a.m. to 10 p.m.. every day of the year.

Post offices are open from 9 a.m. to 6 p.m., Monday to Friday. The main post office in Stockholm is open weekdays 7 a.m. to 9 p.m., Saturday 10 a.m. to 1 p.m., closed Sundays.

Banks are open from 9.30 a.m. to 3 p.m. Monday to Friday (some open again in the afternoon one day a week from 4 to 5.30). The bank at Arlanda Airport is open daily from 7 a.m. to 10 p.m., and the Exchange Bureau at the Central Railway Station from 8 a.m. to 9 p.m.

Museums are usually open between 10 or 11 a.m. and 4 p.m. See also box on page 62.

Chemist's or drugstores are open during normal shopping hours, and a few are on duty nights and Sundays. See HEALTH AND MEDICAL CARE.

L **LANGUAGE.** English is very widely spoken and understood all over Sweden, especially in bigger towns. Children must study English at school from the age of nine. Though Swedish is a pleasant language to hear, you're not likely to find it easy to pronounce. Remember there are three extra letters in the Swedish alphabet—å, ä and ö which appear after the usual 26 letters; something to remember when looking up a name in the telephone book.

The Swedish-English/English-Swedish dictionary and the phrase-book SWEDISH FOR TRAVELLERS published by Berlitz cover practically all the situations you're likely to encounter during a visit to Sweden.

Here are a few words to get you going:

Do you speak English?	**Talar ni engelska?**
Good morning	**God morgon**
Good day/Good afternoon/ Good evening	**Goddag**
Hello (Hi)	**Hej**
Good-bye	**Adjö**
Bye	**Hej då**
Thank you	**Tack**
Good night	**God natt**

LAUNDRY and DRY CLEANING *(tvätt; kemtvätt)*. You can get quick service in the hotels and in certain laundry or dry-cleaning establishments, but prices are high, especially for dry cleaning. If you have a lot of laundry take it to a self-service launderette *(tvättomat* or *tvättbar)*. For addresses look for *Kemisk Tvätt* or *Tvättbarer* under "Tvätt" in the business phone book *Gula Sidorna.*

When will it be ready?	**När kan det bli klart?**
I need it tomorrow morning.	**Jag måste ha det i morgon bitti.**

LOST PROPERTY *(hittegods)*. The main lost property office *(hittegodsexpedition)* is at the police station at Tjärhovsgatan 21 (tel. 769 30 75) in Stockholm, open Monday to Friday from 9 a.m. to 12 noon and 1 to 5 p.m.. Taxi drivers deliver lost articles to this office.

For articles lost on buses and underground trains, contact the Stockholm Local Traffic Office (SL), at the Rådmansgatan underground station from 11 a.m. to 4 p.m. Monday to Friday (between 5 and 7 p.m. on Thursdays), tel. 600 10 00.

MAPS *(karta)*. Road maps of Sweden are on sale at filling stations and bookstores. City maps are available free-of-charge at tourist offices and most hotels, and those with very detailed, indexed street plans are sold in bookstores and in some tobacco shops and kiosks. Falk-Verlag, who provided the maps for this book, publishes a map of Stockholm.

M **MEETING PEOPLE.** See also LANGUAGE. Swedes are not the easiest people in the world to meet, and they're the first to admit it. But once you see through their reserved nature, you'll find some of the friendliest and warmest-natured people on earth. In Stockholm you can meet the locals and other tourists at one of the many dance restaurants.

MONEY MATTERS. Sweden's monetary unit is the *krona* or crown (plural *kronor*), abbreviated kr, or abroad Skr, to distinguish it from the Danish and Norwegian kronor. It is divided into 100 *öre*. Banknotes come in 10, 20, 50, 100, 500, 1,000 and 10,000 kronor; silver coins in 10 (going out of circulation) and 50 öre, 1 krona, 5 and 10 kronor.

Banks and Currency Exchange. Foreign currency can be changed in practically all commercial and savings banks, and the larger hotels and department stores. You get a better rate of exchange for banknotes and traveller's cheques in banks or exchange offices, of course. The bank at Arlanda Airport and the exchange bureau *(växelkontor)* at the Central Railway Station are open every day until evening. See HOURS section.

Most international **credit cards** are welcome—shops and restaurants usually display signs indicating the ones they accept.

Tipping. Service charges are included in hotel and restaurant bills. Gratuities for waiters, hotel maids, tourist guides, and many others in the tourist-related industries, are purely optional. Obviously, a little extra is appreciated for special services rendered, but it isn't expected. In a few areas, however, the habit is slightly more engrained:

Cloakroom attendant	charges posted or 3.50 kr
Hairdresser/Barber	optional
Hotel porter, per bag	3–4 kr (optional)
Lavatory attendant	3 kr
Taxi driver	10%

Sales tax. Called Moms, value added tax is a sales tax on all goods and services. Residents of countries outside Scandinavia will be refunded most of the tax on purchases made during their stay in Sweden (see p. 80 for details).

NEWSPAPERS and MAGAZINES *(tidning; tidskrift)*. Foreign language newspapers, including the *International Herald Tribune* and leading English papers, as well as a wide variety of magazines, are on sale at the Central Railway Station, airport shops, in some hotels, tobacco shops and kiosks in central Stockholm.

PHOTOGRAPHY *(fotografering)*. All popular types of cameras and film are available in Sweden at good prices—in fact cameras are a very good buy.

Colour film development usually takes one week, although a number of shops in the centre of town offer either a one-hour or two-day service.

Some museums allow visitors to take photos, but never with a tripod or flash.

I'd like a film for this camera.	**Jag skulle vilja ha en film till den här kameran.**
black-and-white film	**svartvit film**
colour prints	**färgfilm**
colour slides	**färgfilm för diabilder**
How long will it take to develop (and print) this film?	**Hur lång tid tar det att framkalla (och göra kopior av) den här filmen?**

POLICE *(polis)*. The Stockholm police patrol cars are marked POLIS. Members of the force are invariably courteous and helpful to tourists, and all of them speak some English, so don't hesitate to ask them questions or directions. Police headquarters is at Agnegatan 33–37 in Stockholm, tel. 769 30 00.

Meter maids, dressed in light-blue uniforms, issue parking tickets—and they do a thorough job.

On the motorways and roads routine spot checks are quite frequent.

PUBLIC HOLIDAYS *(helgdag)*. Banks, offices and shops close on public holidays in Sweden, but many cinemas, restaurants, museums, some food shops and tourist attractions remain open. On the day before a holiday, most shops close early. On Christmas Eve virtually everything is closed.

Movable dates: Good Friday *(Långfredagen)*, Easter *(Påskdagen)*, Easter Monday *(Annandag påsk)*, Ascension *(Kristi himmelsfärdsdag)*, Whit-Sunday/Monday *(Pingstdagen/Annandag pingst)*.

P

New Year's Day	*Nyårsdagen*	January 1
Twelfth Day	*Trettondagen*	January 6
May Day	*Första Maj*	May 1
Midsummer Day	*Midsommardagen*	On the Saturday that falls between June 20 and 26
All Saints' Day	*Allhelgonadagen*	On the Saturday which falls between October 31–November 6
Christmas Day/ Boxing Day	*Juldagen/ Annandag jul*	December 25, 26

PUBLIC TRANSPORT*. Stockholm has very efficient and modern underground or subway *(tunnelbana)* and bus systems which make it easy to get around the city and its environs from about 5 a.m. (a little later on Sundays) to 2 a.m. Underground stations are indicated by a blue "T". Maps can be referred to in the station or on the train.

Tickets are valid on all means of transport for one hour from the time they are stamped. They can be bought from bus drivers, at underground station booths or at Press Agency *(Pressbyrån)* news-stands in cards of 18 units, which are stamped according to the distance travelled. Children and pensioners (senior citizens) pay half-price.

Special one- and three-day tourist tickets are also sold in the Pressbyrån kiosks.

Tourist buses circulate between the major attractions.

Taxis*. You can flag them down anywhere in Stockholm or find them at stands marked *Taxi* (the biggest is in front of the Central Railway Station). The sign *Ledig* (vacant) lighted up indicates when a taxi is available; but cabs are difficult to find during rush hours and on rainy days. If you want to book one in advance call 150400 or ask your hotel receptionist to reserve for you. For tipping see MONEY MATTERS.

R

RADIO and TV. Sveriges Radio (The Swedish Broadcasting Corporation) has a monopoly on all radio and television programmes transmitted in Sweden. There are three nationwide radio networks and two TV channels which are financed through licence fees. News in English is broadcast in summer. For the schedule, refer to the local papers.

RELIGIOUS SERVICES. About 95% of Sweden's native-born population are Lutheran Evangelical, the state-established church. Roman Catholics are estimated at about 60.000 and those of Jewish and other faiths are also represented. Non-Lutheran services are held in the following churches (services are at 11 a.m. Sunday):

Anglican: Anglican Church, Strandvägen 76, tel. 661 22 23.

Catholic: Marie Bebådelsekyrkan (The Church of the Blessed Annunciation), Linnégatan 79, tel. 661 69 36.

Jewish: The Great Synagogue (conservative), Wahrendorffsgatan 3A, tel. 23 51 60.

STOCKHOLM CARD* *Stockholmskortet* offers visitors the chance to see the city at a fair price. Similar in appearance to a credit card, it allows the holder free entry to about 60 museums, castles and other sights, free public transport, including sightseeing buses and boats, reduced-price excursions to Drottningholm Palace, free parking (provided a special parking card is obtained at the time of purchase), etc. Used to the full, it represents a considerable bargain. The pass is valid from one to three days. It is available only through local tourist offices at Sweden House, the Central Station and numerous other places.

TIME DIFFERENCES. Sweden follows Central European Time (GMT + 1). In summer, the Swedes put their clocks ahead an hour.

TOILETS *(toalett).* Public facilities are located in underground (subway) stations, department stores and some of the bigger streets, squares and parks. They are often labelled with symbols for men and women, or marked *WC, Damer/Herrar* (Ladies/Gentlemen) or simply *D/H.* Some have slots for coins or an attendant to give towels and soap (for a small charge), but most are free.

TOURIST INFORMATION. There are more than 300 non-profit tourist offices in Sweden. They have a very good selection of brochures and maps of their respective regions, and can provide you with information on sightseeing, excursions, restaurants, hotels, camping, sports, etc. In Sweden tourist offices *(turistbyrå)* are indicated by the international sign (a white "i" on a green background).

T   In Stockholm the Sweden House (Sverigehuset) groups several tourist organizations at the same address and telephone number. There's also a library and book shop there with information about Sweden in foreign languages, open on weekdays.

The following addresses and telephone numbers should be helpful when you plan a visit to Sweden or when you're in Stockholm:

Sweden House, Hamngatan 27, near Kungsträdgården, tel. 789 20 00. This building houses the offices of the Stockholm Information Service, with the Tourist Centre, and the Swedish Institute *(Svenska Institutet)*.

Sweden Travel Shop offers information on parts of Sweden other than Stockholm and can book travel tickets and accommodation. Located at Stureplan 8, they cannot be reached by phone.

Hotellcentralen, Stockholm's official accommodation service, Central Railway Station (lower ground floor), tel. 24 08 80 and at Arlanda Airport.

"What's on today", automatic telephone tourist information in English: 22 18 40.

The Swedish Tourist Board also has representatives in the following countries:

Great Britain: Swedish National Tourist Office, 29-31 Oxford Street, London W1R 1RE, tel. (071) 437 5816-18.

U.S.A.: Scandinavian National Tourist Offices, 655 Third Avenue, 18th floor, New York, NY 10017; tel.: (212) 949-2333.

Scandinavian Tourist Board, Denmark-Sweden, 150 North Michigan Avenue, Suite 2110, Chicago, IL 60601; tel.: (312) 899-1121.

Scandinavian Tourist Board, Denmark–Sweden, 8929 Wilshire Boulevard, Suite 300, Beverly Hills, CA 90211; tel.: (213) 854-1549.

TRAINS* *(tåg)*. The Swedish State Railways *(Statens Järnvägar* or *SJ)* operate an extensive network of rail lines, with more than 90% of the traffic carried on electric trains. It's a very efficient railway system, with trains leaving Stockholm for most big towns every hour or two. From the Central Station *(Centralstationen)* you can reach virtually every part of Sweden by rail, and there are direct links to Copenhagen, Berlin and other European cities.

Fares are based on a "sliding scale"—the longer the journey the less the price per kilometre. Children under 6 travel free. Seat reservations are often compulsory, especially on express trains *(expresståg)*. Enquire about the various discount plans available.

Inter-city coaches *(snabbussar)*. Express buses can be used instead of (or in addition to) trains to many places in Sweden. Although there are private companies. Swedish Railways operates a low-priced. efficient coach system between towns, cities and outlying areas. For schedules and bookings check with the office at Cityterminalen, tel. 23 71 90. The branch offices for state-run coach and rail are indicated by signs SJ Resebyrå, and tickets can be purchased in any railway station.

SOME USEFUL EXPRESSIONS

yes/no	**ja/nej**
please/thank you	**var snäll och/tack**
excuse me	**ursäkta mig**
how long/how far	**hur länge/hur långt**
yesterday/today/tomorrow	**igår/idag/i morgon**
day/week/month/year	**dag/vecka/månad/år**
left/right	**vänster/höger**
up/down	**uppe/nere**
good/bad	**bra/dålig**
right/wrong	**rätt/fel**
big/small	**stor/liten**
cheap/expensive	**billig/dyr**
hot/cold	**varm/kall**
old/new	**gammal/ny**
open/closed	**öppen/stängd**
entrance/exit	**ingång/utgång**
pull/push	**drag/skjut**
permitted/not permitted	**tillåten/förbjuden**
occupied/vacant	**upptagen/ledig**
I don't understand.	**Jag förstår inte.**
Please write it down.	**Kan ni skriva det?**
What does this mean?	**Vad betyder det här?**
Could you help me, please?	**Kan ni hjälpa mig?**
I'd like…	**Jag skulle vilja ha…**
How much is it?	**Hur mycket kostar det?**

Index

An asterisk (*) next to a page number indicates a map reference. In Swedish, å, ä and ö are considered separate letters and come at the end of the alphabet—but to avoid confusion, we have integrated them in the following listing.

INDEX

127